AF242459

"This book is an exposé of the bail bond business. It is an intimate and in-depth look at the life of a young Jewish woman coming of age in Southern California who was inadvertently thrusted into a male-dominated industry at a time in history when women were assertively seeking to be respected as valuable human beings with intellectual capital and physical stamina. It was a time when women were demanding to be seen as being comparable to their male counterparts. Chickie Levanthal, a young lady struggling with the trials, tribulations, and triumphs of life, takes the reader on an entertaining yet instructive journey where the greatest teaching is of how determination, ingenuity, consistency, and a little bit of 'hutzspa' can yield significant benefits. I highly recommend this book to everyone, particularly to middle school, high school, and college students, and to people interested in reinventing their lives. Among other things, the reader will see how to incorporate their originality in all they do, so that they may meet success anchored in their own authenticity."

—Helen Easterling Williams, EdD
Dean Emeritus-Graduate School of
Education and Psychology, Pepperdine University

"I loved this book! I didn't want Chickie's stories to end. Chickie brings class, compassion, and grit to the bail bond world—she is an example all to herself."

—Stacy D. Phillips
Nationally recognized and certified family law specialist,
partner Blank Rome LLP

"I first met Chickie when I was a defense attorney on the federal indigent panel in Los Angeles. She was on the stand trying to post a bond for a defendant. Afterwards, I told her that she was very good and professional. I recommended her to my friends on the panel and the Federal Defenders. We met in my office one day and I said to her, 'If we could make $5,000 a month, we'd be successful.' We both got there, but I became a Federal Immigration Judge, and I told her that she still made more than me. She is a great lady and we are still friends."

—The Honorable Anna Ho, retired

CHICKIE!

THE WOMAN WHO CRASHED THE ALL-MALE BAIL BOND INDUSTRY

Chickie Leventhal

Flint Hills Publishing

Cover design by Amy Albright

Author photograph by Steven Cohn

⫲Flint Hills Publishing
Topeka, Kansas
Tucson, Arizona
www.flinthillspublishing.com

Printed in the U.S.A.

This book is a work of memoir.
While the events described are true to the best
of the author's recollections, this work reflects the author's
subjective perspective and understanding of those events.

Paperback Book ISBN: 978-1-966323-62-4
Hardcover Book ISBN: 978-1-966323-63-1
Electronic Book ISBN: 978-1-966323-64-8

Library of Congress Control Number: 2026907088

DEDICATED TO MY DEAR SON MITCH,
WITHOUT WHOM THERE WOULD BE NO
CHICKIE'S BAIL BONDS.

Dear Reader,

Thank you for picking up my book.

Chickie! The Woman Who Crashed the All-Male Bail Bond Industry, was written not only to entertain, but more importantly, to carry the message that anyone can succeed regardless of their circumstances. I went from a poor kid raised in Boyle Heights, Los Angeles, to living the life I could only have dreamed of. I have done this with hard work, dedication, and integrity.

Enjoy what you are about to experience, every word of which is true.

With love and compassion,

Chickie
May 2026

CONTENTS

FOREWORD
BY
ROBERT L. SHAPIRO

I am a firm believer in our Constitution and the laws of our great nation. The United States criminal justice system places significant value on protecting the innocent—and that is where my professional allegiance has resided since I was admitted to the State Bar of California in 1969. Central to our country's legal ideology—and one I support with strong conviction—is that it is better to let a guilty person go free than to convict an innocent person.

Posting a bail bond can be a tricky business, especially if the accused is facing a murder charge and the bail amount is set at a steep one million dollars or more. This can be a daunting experience for anyone—even when the accused is wealthy or has celebrity status. Whereas many judges are fair and logical in determining bail amount, others can be idiosyncratic or overly severe.

This is why I choose to call upon the best professional assistance available to prepare and assemble all of the paperwork, sort out who is providing collateral (the client, a friend, a family member, etc.), verifying acceptable collateral, and then handling the actual posting of the bond.

After all of that is completed to the court's satisfaction and my client is released, my legal team can build the defense strategy working face-to-face with our client.

When I need a bail bond agent to obtain my client's release, I don't google names on the internet or choose from the myriad of bail bond agency offices located outside of every jail and many courthouses. I pick up the phone and dial one person: Chickie Leventhal.

As people who know me well can attest, I only work with people I am one hundred percent confident I can trust. I've always kept my word in all of my business and personal relationships, and I expect my business associates and clients to do the same. I implicitly trust Chickie and am certain I can count on her for anything—no matter what needs and circumstances may arise.

The most important call I make upon being retained in a criminal case is to Chickie, as she is always there to give me a jump start on the case.

For years Chickie has proven herself to be a reliable trooper and an unquestioning team player.

She treats everyone with equal respect—clients, their families, district attorneys, judges, criminal defense attorneys, jail and court personnel—which enables everyone to work at a professional level and provide dignity to what might otherwise become an uncom-fortable situation.

When the stakes are high, speed is the top priority. Chickie will drop everything to serve the needs of her clients. She is ready, willing, and able to meet them at any hour of the day and at the location of their choosing.

What truly makes Chickie stand out is her innate understanding of the legal process. She lives and breathes the concept of innocent until proven guilty and is unflinching and even zealous when it comes to supporting her clients.

She is as comfortable posting bail for a person accused of a minor crime as she is for high-profile or recognizable clients defending themselves against charges of committing a serious crime, such as murder, and never is there the slightest trace of judgment or condescension on her part.

Thanks to this book, you will see what it takes to be a great bail bond agent— ensuring a client's attendance at trial even though they may decide to skip town and vanish forever off the face of the earth.

This book is a delightful read and has been a long time coming. As I read Chickie's open casebook, I found myself laughing out loud at the cast of characters she encountered over the years. Conversely, I felt emotionally moved by the horrific situations some people found themselves in. The one thing that comes across loud and clear in every story is how much Chickie cares about people and her clients, and the great lengths she will go for them.

Chickie has underscored the vital role of bail bond agents in the judicial process and has eloquently demonstrated how they have been unjustly mischaracterized and misunderstood and maligned over the years.

Robert L. Shapiro

PROLOGUE

It's four o'clock in the morning and I'm sitting in a booth at Denny's Restaurant on the outskirts of downtown Los Angeles. A disheveled man is sitting across from me, weary and somewhat distraught, absolutely drenched in "California Sunshine," the season's rain that had already drowned the parking lot outside. It's a look I am very familiar with.

He pushes an envelope stuffed full of money toward me. Twenty thousand dollars to bail his friend out of jail.

Without opening the envelope, I confidently place it in my briefcase. A puzzled look comes across my client's face.

"Aren't you going to count it?" he asks.

Smiling, I shake my head no. I know I don't have to, that all of the twenty thousand dollars is there.

Receiving a large sum of money from a stranger in an envelope in the dark of night might sound unusual to most people—but to me, it's just another day at the office.

My name is Chickie Leventhal, owner of Chickie's Bail Bonds. For 37 years I have provided my professional services to many of the most despicable, fascinating, and wonderful human beings, some of whom I now call friends.

Los Angeles is a city known for glitz and glamor, full of vibrant characters and stories. Despite being called the city of dreams, many people instead find heartbreak and desperation—getting themselves caught up in the criminal justice system.

The job of a bail-bond agent is to ensure that the arrestee does not remain in custody unnecessarily and to know that the accused is not automatically guilty. Only the court can make that determination. My job is to make certain that the arrestee shows up to trial to face the charges. In other words, to ensure that justice will be served.

The bail-bond industry and the people involved have always had a horrible reputation. On television and in movies they're depicted as the scum of the earth; they're all heartless, morally bankrupt thieves.

And it's always a man—one that's overweight, unshaven, and slovenly with a chewed-up stogie hanging out of his mouth.

And here I was, a nice middle-aged Jewish mother with manicured nails, a sharp business suit, bright red hair, and standing at five-foot-four-inches tall (if I'm on my toes). My claim to fame is that I created the first female-owned bail-bond agency in Los Angeles, There were no bondswomen, only bondsmen.

In a male-dominated industry in one of the biggest cities in the world, I established a reputation as the best in the business by being trustworthy, reliable, and by working harder than my all-male competition.

When celebrities and other high-profile individuals get arrested—it's time to call Chickie. When top attorneys want the most professional in the business—it's time to call Chickie.

Our system of justice is based on the presumption of *innocence* which means everyone is innocent until proven guilty in a court of law. We are all equal in the eyes of the law, and everybody deserves bail, with few exceptions.

To me, the job of a bail-bond agent is so much more than paperwork and posting bail for a defendant. When I meet with the accused's family and/or friends, they are looking to me to help have their loved one released from custody. I offer them compassion and understanding. I explain how the system works and what I can and cannot do.

Everyone who knows me has heard me say that the majority of my clients are not criminals. This is a true statement. In the majority of cases these are just people who have made a really stupid mistake. In the heat of a bad moment perceptions can get distorted and all sense of right and wrong goes out the window. Next comes the sound of the jail cell door, slamming shut behind them with a resounding metal clang.

And it can happen to anyone.

My life did not start out in this direction. But after a series of unpredictable events, I found this to be my calling. I created Chickie's Bail Bonds in 1984 when I was 50 years old—an age when most women were slowing down, certainly not starting a new career. It was a man's world. Most women didn't have careers, they had jobs, possibly being a secretary—for a man, of course.

I didn't have the luxury of following along with those sexist considerations. The life I had laid out before me changed dramatically when my husband became ill. I had a choice: I could feel sorry for myself, or I could get to work. I decided to get to work.

Working in this industry has opened my eyes to a whole world of different kinds of people in all walks of life. Young and old, from poverty to great wealth, and from uneducated to doctors. People with different backgrounds and ethnicities. There's really not that much difference. We all just want to put food on the table. We all feel pain. We all want love. We are all human.

-1-
THE DAY MY LIFE CHANGED

Fred's illness started innocuously enough.

Fred worked in Los Angeles and fought the 405 Freeway home every day. He was an angry bear when he stormed into the house—until he discovered jogging. On his way home, he would drive to the local high school track where after running around for an hour, he became a pussycat. What a welcome change!

After one of his nightly runs, Fred came home with a strange look on his face. He told me he was having trouble with his left foot. "It just won't lift up like it's supposed to," he said. He showed me, and his foot definitely wasn't working right. Although I was concerned, I remember hoping it was just a temporary thing.

"Foot flap," was what one doctor called it. It sounded simple, but what was the solution? The doctor's *brilliant* advice? "Walk instead of run."

The year was 1980. Fred was my husband of 28 years. We had been together since I was a teenager. He was an engineer for the Los Angeles County Road department and didn't make a lot of money, but we were doing all right.

Throughout our marriage Fred insisted he was the breadwinner and that it wasn't necessary for me to work. He wanted me to be the good little homemaker, but that wasn't me. Of course I wanted to be at home when our two wonderful children were little, but once they were off to school, I followed them right out the door. To appease Fred, I took part-time secretarial positions and continued pulling the weeds from the garden he was so proud of having created. In those days men ruled the roost. That was the norm.

Despite the trouble with his foot, Fred cautiously continued jogging. He soon, however, developed other difficulties. Fred's voice would become so hoarse by the end of the day, it was hard to hear him. I thought it was just the stress of his job. *Maybe he's just hollering at work.*

In the days before the internet, we were completely reliant on doctors—several of whom could not identify Fred's condition—until one finally did.

Multiple sclerosis, explained the doctor, is a degenerative disease; incurable. Depending on how the symptoms progress, it could cause Fred to be confined to a wheelchair one day.

To say I was terrified fails to adequately describe the situation.

When the doctor came out from behind his desk, we were shocked to see how he dragged his legs, using two long sticks to balance himself. Obviously, the doctor was also a victim of MS *Could this be Fred one day?*

Although I was grateful to finally get some answers, I had even more questions. It was a quiet drive home. The words "progressive," "degenerative," and "incurable" kept racing through my mind.

As I lay in bed that night, I started assessing options, again finding more questions than answers. How long would Fred be able to work? Would I have to support our family? How could I do that on a secretary's salary?

There I was, almost 50 years old, unemployed, with a husband who had been given a frightening prognosis for a virtually unknown disease.

I thought my life was over.

What I didn't know was that my life had just begun.

Throughout my life, I have prided myself on being able to turn a negative into a positive. No matter the odds stacked against me, I always found my way, focusing on the things that I could control.

My mother would say "I never worry about Chickie—she always has a smile on her face."

Chickie is a pretty unusual name. Very few people know that my real name is Sophie. I was named for my mother's oldest dearest sister who died early in life. It's Jewish tradition to name children after those who have passed to honor and remember them. It's a lovely name. It means wisdom.

When my mother brought me home from the hospital, she said I cried like a chicken and called me her "little chickie." Little did she know her cute nickname for me would become the name I would use to make my mark in life.

One of my earliest memories was being late to my first-grade class. Refusing to hear my excuses, my teacher punished my tardiness by having me sit in a rocking chair in front of the class. My dear friend Lorraine watched in shock—an incident she still vividly remembers to this day.

As I slowly climbed into that chair, I felt the heat from my beet-red face. I was mortified and wished the ground would swallow me up. I pretended not to be upset as I was forced to listen to the students who sang, "Here comes Sophie, here comes Sophie, late again, late again."

The name "Chickie" was a welcome reprieve.

I liked that Chickie was my special name. A name that nobody else had, one given to me by my role model: my mother.

No one had a stronger work ethic than my mother. She worked two jobs and never missed a day of work. My mother dragged herself to work with a broken leg; once with 103 temperature from pneumonia; always able to push aside these kinds of "distractions." It was as if she wouldn't acknowledge anything that might get in the way of providing for her family.

I was too young to remember anything about the relationship between my parents, but my mother would tell my sister and me that every time she asked my father a question, he would respond with the same three little words: "Don't bother me." Not a good thing to say to such a headstrong woman.

"Joe," my mother warned him, "if I hear you say, 'Don't bother me' one more time, I'm leaving you." Sure enough, he replied, "Don't bother me."

My mother left, taking my older sister Reba and me to California. It was during the height of the Great Depression, a time when a wife leaving her husband was unheard of … except for my mother.

One has to wonder how she could have abandoned her Midwest support system and raised two children on her own, but my mother had a secret weapon. She had graduated from bookkeeping school at sixteen years of age and was confident she could support her family.

We didn't have much money, but my mother never let us know it. We didn't have anything fancy like a dishwasher, but my mother made sure we had what we needed and we were never hungry. We were secular Jews, meaning that we didn't observe the Sabbath or keep Kosher. However, we celebrated the major holidays like Passover, Rosh Hashanah, and Yom Kippur. I remember my mother stopping on her way home from work to buy traditional foods for holiday dinners, typically, a jar of gefilte fish and a chicken ready to cook. After dinner my mother would wash the dishes while I dried, and that's when she shared her life's wisdom with me, sharing her thoughts on the importance of the "Three P's."

Perseverance meant staying the course no matter the obstacle. My mother set the example for this every day of her life, going to work even with a broken leg.

Personality was being able to stand out in a crowd. My older sister Reba was gorgeous, with flowing black hair and hazel eyes. She didn't have to worry about personality. I, on the other hand, was short, chubby, and shy with a penchant for Hershey bars. From the age of five I had piano lessons. My mother firmly believed a musical skill would give me personality. Oh, how I hated practicing piano every day while my sister Reba would be off charming boys.

The third P was *profession.* Something to fall back on should circumstances ever arise, as they did in her life. I diligently studied typing and shorthand in high school, and during summer vacations my mother would take me to her office where the boss complimented me on my skills in answering their telephones. My career choice was made at age thirteen! I would be a secretary!

-2-
EVERY JOURNEY STARTS WITH THE FIRST STEP

While motherhood was deeply fulfilling, I knew that it wasn't my major calling in life. There was something out there just waiting for me to discover it, something I would be compelled to do, something where I could make a difference.

Fred's MS seemed to be creating new symptoms almost every day. He was no longer able to jog and was losing the feeling in his hands. He said that if he put his hand in his pocket, he didn't know whether he was going to pull out a comb or a dime. On the outside Fred seemed like he was doing okay, but he really wasn't. He was suffering. He just never talked about it.

Dinner was cooking in the oven as I sat down at our dining room table. I had saved every penny I earned working as a secretary during our first year of marriage while Fred was serving in Korea, enough to furnish our first small apartment. This antique table was one of my favorite things, more than just a dining room table. It was where we celebrated happy occasions with family and friends. I opened the *Los Angeles Times* advertising section to "Help Wanted." The same words repeated over and over on the page, staring me in the face:

HELP WANTED. SECRETARY.

I closed the newspaper.

Absolutely not.

I couldn't fathom the idea of going back to being a secretary. That's where I had started when I was 17 years old. Type this, file that, answer the phone, sort these documents—always being told what to do by someone else. After years of hard work, I had finally shaken my secretary moniker when I became the assistant vice president of a surety insurance company with a company car, a secretary of my own, and a staff of eight women to supervise. It was my dream job until the company crashed and the office I was so proud of ceased to exist.

I didn't have the time or patience to fight tooth and nail up the corporate ladder again and I had yet to see any ads looking for an assistant vice president.

Before I met Marvin Byron, I had no idea what the word "bail" meant. The attorney husband of my dear friend, Flo Medove, approached me about returning to the workforce. Jack convinced me that my son Mitch, at three years old, was old enough for nursery school. He begged me to help out his business associate, not mentioning the type of business.

Marvin's office wasn't in a great part of Los Angeles, and I was concerned about driving my Volkswagen on the freeway from West Covina to LA, but I relished going back to work after three years of being a stay-at-home mom.

It wasn't much of an office at all—it was more like a trash container. A tiny living room in someone's duplex with a worn-out couch, a couple of mismatched desks, and some folding chairs. I won't even discuss the atrocity that was the bathroom.

Since it was my first day, Marvin sat me down to go over the basics of the bail-bond industry.

"Bail was created to allow one accused of a crime to remain out of custody pending the outcome of the charges brought against him or her."

This made sense when I thought about it. In the United States an individual is "innocent until proven guilty." Why should someone who is innocent be locked up?

Marvin continued as he marched around the beat-up couch, being careful to keep his attractive suit away from the less-than-immaculate furniture. "Bail-bond agents are licensed by the Department of Insurance through a surety insurance company and are able to post bail on behalf of the accused." Marvin saw the confused look on my face and explained that the word "bail" is the dollar amount set by the court to guarantee that the accused will show up to court to have their case adjudicated.

He stopped for a moment, knowing I needed more of an explanation.

"In order to become a bail bond agent, the applicant is vetted by an insurance company and licensed by the California Department of Insurance after passing a fairly difficult test, although nowhere as difficult as what a prospective lawyer is subject to, but no walk in the park either."

Marvin went on to explain that collateral is an asset that can be turned into cash with which to pay the court, should the defendant fail to appear. A family member, friend, or associate accepts that financial responsibility as well as paying the ten percent premium for the posting of the bond.

Well! This sounded a lot more interesting than my usual secretarial work.

It was then that I noticed one of the walls in the main room had an odd-looking greenish stain. Marvin saw me staring at it and casually remarked that one of his bail-bond agents had hurled a plate of guacamole during a fit of rage. His name was Stu, a former prize fighter with anger management issues.

This was *definitely* a lot more interesting than my usual secretarial work.

Despite the unkempt office, Marvin dressed like a gentleman and was respected wherever he went. He criticized other bail agents whom he felt were not a good representation of the industry. Most of them wore tank tops or ripped T-shirts and rarely combed their hair. "How is the court going to respect us if we don't respect ourselves enough to dress properly?" I heard Marvin exclaim more than once.

At Byron's Bail Bonds I did not deal directly with the issuance of bonds. Without a bail license my responsibilities were limited to paperwork. On one occasion, however, I did cross the line. Marvin Byron was out of the office when a client appeared with a pile of cash. The agent in the office and I took the cash, counted it, and gave the client a receipt.

I thought Marvin would blow his top when he recounted the cash—*we* had inadvertently given the client a receipt for more money than we had received. Needless to say, I was never involved in counting cash again.

It was through Marvin that I was introduced to the movers and shakers in the industry: Celes King, Dan Majors, and Irving Glasser. Along with Marvin, they were the pioneers of the industry who put bail bonds on the map. When the California Legislature threatened to outlaw bail, these are the gentlemen who personally went to Sacramento and saved the California Bail Bond industry.

Richard Savage, a general agent for a surety insurance company, was an equal opportunity bigot. It didn't matter whether you were Black, Hispanic, Jewish, or a woman—he had the same contempt for us all.

I had met Mr. Savage through Marvin Byron. At the time, he was on his best behavior, and after I left Byron's Bail Bonds, he offered me a secretarial position with his general agency—meaning I would be working at a higher level in the industry.

We were never allowed to call him Richard; we could only address him as Mr. Savage. True to his name, he would sling offensive comments all day long at his staff. He'd browbeat all of his employees, moving from one desk to the next like a tornado, leaving a trail of devastation in his wake. It was the 70s—there was no human resources department to complain to.

Richard's partner, attorney Spencer Douglas, wasn't much better. At one point, Spencer hired his neighbor to work in the office and told me that one of my duties was to make sure his neighbor stayed in the office when Spencer was out because Spencer was off screwing his employee/neighbor's wife.

I was devastated when, three years into the job, Richard Savage fired me—until I learned why. His previous secretary, now ready to return to work, performed duties not of a secretarial nature. Duties I was not willing to undertake. My friend Sandy, the bookkeeper, kept me apprised.

After Richard Savage and Spencer Douglas had had enough of each other, Spencer left and opened the Southern California office for the respected Midwest surety—Allied Fidelity Insurance Company—and offered me the position of head of bail operations. As much as I disrespected Spencer, I was thrilled to be moving up again in the industry. My joy was dampened when I learned Spencer had given the huge window office to a man with a lower-ranking job title than me. It didn't matter that he had little between his ears. What mattered was what he had in his trousers.

When Bill Rowe, head of Allied Fidelity, learned that Spencer had been using his employees to work on his political campaign instead of working in the office, he fired Spencer replacing him with Jim Garske, a very welcome change.

Allied Fidelity's well-loved owner, Bill Rowe, was an aficionado of stunt flying and frequently participated in air shows. One weekend he invited all of the top people in the company to a special air show. After his impressive demonstration, the group boarded two small planes for their return home.

Mr. Rowe, still eager to impress his employees, attempted to maneuver his plane around the other. Misjudging the distance, he caused both planes to come crashing down in flames.

All of the top people at Allied Fidelity perished with Mr. Rowe that day, signifying the end of an era. It was a horrible thing which took place thousands of miles away from our office in Los Angeles. Still, our office was completely devastated at the terrible news. In the insurance business no one loves anyone … but everyone loved Bill Rowe.

With the collapse of Allied Fidelity, Jim Garske created the West Coast branch of Cotton Belt Insurance Company. When he and his wife, Patty, decided they didn't like living in Southern California they made plans to move to Santa Rosa. Jim appointed me his assistant vice president, leaving me in charge of the office and the eight women employees; the one male employee refused to answer to a woman and joined Jim in Santa Rosa. The position came with all kinds of perks. I had my own secretary, Carole Power, and my very own company car! What a thrill it was to go to the showroom and select a brand-new sparkling pearl white, four-door Ford!

When Carole learned I had never had a Christmas stocking, she was appalled. The next Christmas she presented me with a hand-knit bright green stocking decorated with a jolly red Santa, a white Star of David, and the thoughtful greeting on the bottom: OY VEY! I loved it. Each year I hang my stocking and think of my thoughtful friend.

The women working in the office were all young without court experience. When I asked my agent George Cameron if one of his sons might be interested in checking courts for me, he said, "No, but my daughter would." And so began my life-long relationship with George's daughter, Verlene, whom I introduce as my daughter and my kids consider sister.

I was in charge of the Southern California operation, and part of my job was getting to know my bail agents whom occasionally I would take to lunch. They were all nice enough, but they didn't present themselves very well. I remember one bail agent whom I took to a nice Italian restaurant. As hard as I tried to make small talk, all I could hear was the sound of his spaghetti being slurped through his toothless mouth. Taking George Cameron to lunch in honor of his birthday was much more pleasant—until I realized I had left my wallet in the office. George paid for his own birthday lunch—and never let me forget it!

As I got to know bail agents, it became clear to me that there weren't many of them who were making a great deal of money—they were just surviving. It certainly didn't seem like much of a career.

One exception was George Cameron. He was unlike any other bail agent. George was a handsome Black gentleman who wore three-piece suits and drove a brand-new Cadillac. When he entered the office, all the girls swooned.

George had been a successful bail agent for many years and was someone I admired and trusted. He never treated me differently because I was a woman; he treated me with respect and had confidence in me that I hadn't yet discovered in myself. For years he would preach to me that I should become an agent. "You've got to get yourself a license, Chickie," he'd say.

I was flattered but told him I already had a job. Besides, I didn't want to be just some bail agent. I would have wanted to be a bail agent like *him* and that could take years.

As I finished setting the dining room table, I found myself lost in thought. I didn't have years. Fred certainly didn't either. It all seemed so impossible.

I placed the bulky ceramic casserole dish on the dining room table just as I heard the front door open.

Fred was home from work. 5:30 on the dot.

"What's for dinner?" he asked as the front door closed behind him. Even when I worked, I had always made sure that when Fred came home there was food prepared on the dining room table. "Tuna casserole."

My son Mitch still talks about the tuna casserole.

There was a faint sound of disappointment in Fred's voice. "Again?"

Since Fred's diagnosis we had been tightening our belts. Economizing was something I was used to in our marriage. When the times called for it, I had learned to be creative about stretching a dollar. I could turn a cheap steak into a stew, leftover ground beef into a taco salad, or a can of tuna into a casserole. I was determined to create a beautiful life regardless of our financial situation.

We couldn't afford expensive art, so I poured over magazines for photos of fruit and vegetables to mount on our kitchen wall. I bought fabric and created a pretty kitchen window shade. I didn't let the fact that I couldn't sew stop me. I just marched over to the hardware store and bought a staple gun and some glue. I did the most with what I had, and I always found a solution. Always.

I placed a cloth napkin in Fred's lap and served him a piece of tuna casserole. Through all our strife my main concern was making my husband happy. Giving him a wide smile I asked, "How was your day?"

"Oh, fine, fine." Fred took a bite and seemed to be enjoying it, and for a moment, everything seemed normal. From the outside we were just a normal married couple having dinner together with our son, as if my mind wasn't caught up thinking about what our future held.

I needed a successful career and I needed it *now*.

I thought about all of the successful people I had met over the years. People in the bail-bond industry like George Cameron, Marvin Byron, Celes King, and others who had achieved financial stability and didn't have to answer to anybody. I wanted to be just like them.

They were all successful, but they were all successful *men*.

All but one.

"I'm Nancy Reynolds, Reynolds as in Wrap," said a striking older woman as she greeted me with an outstretched hand. It was the late 70s and Nancy had just moved into the condo next door to us in Santa Monica.

Shaking her hand, I couldn't help noticing how perfectly put together she was. She dressed impeccably and not one hair was out of place. She later confided in me that she had her hair cut precisely every three weeks so that she always looked the same.

Nancy had moved from Sacramento where she was the front man for Ronald Reagan, the eight years he was Governor of California, and she was now working to get him into the White House. Here was a woman achieving the highest level of success in a male-dominated political world who carried herself with a level of confidence I had never seen in a woman.

Nancy would entertain in her next-door condo, and I would observe people that I recognized from television, with names I had read about in the newspaper. These were smart, political people who would gather in Nancy's living room, listening to her say things like, "Well then, how are we going to get Ronnie into the White House?"

Nancy opened my eyes to a new world, and I drank it all in. Nancy had real power and influence. Most importantly, she had the ability to make a difference.

Nancy was also working with Ronald Reagan's wife, Nancy Reagan, helping returning prisoners of war. I was introduced to Lt. Colonel Hayden Lockheart, who had made history as the longest held prisoner of the Vietnam war and was featured on the cover of *LIFE* magazine, bending down to shake the hand of his eight-year-old son, a son whom he had just met. Hearing his story and how Nancy had helped him, made me realize I didn't just want a job. I wanted to help people.

I thought back to the "Three Ps" my mother taught me: personality, perseverance, and profession. Yes, "profession!"

I know what I want to do. I want to start my own business.

I knew that the only thing worse than making a bad decision was making no decision at all. I lugged our huge *Yellow Pages* phone directory onto our dining room table, madly tearing through it, checking out the competition. There were pages upon pages of long-established bail-bond agencies: *Al's Bail Bonds ... Larry's Bail Bonds ... Rick the Bailman ... Fast Eddie's Bail Bonds ...*

Not one woman in sight.

I knew in that moment that was how I was going to stand out from the crowd!

The only problem was that I didn't have any money. The other bail agents had those huge *Yellow Pages* ads that cost thousands of dollars—much more than I could afford. Doubt immediately started to creep in. How could I compete? Not only could I not afford an ad, I also couldn't afford to rent an office!

I picked up the telephone and dialed George Cameron's number. If anyone knew how I could start a bail bond company with limited resources, it would be him. He picked up on the first ring.

I told him that I had my my bail license and wanted to create my own business. He was excited that I was finally following through on his suggestion from years ago.

He said the business was really about referrals and gave me the one piece of advice that would change my life: "All you need are a few good attorneys."

A light bulb went off. If I could get a steady flow of clients through attorney *referrals*, I would be able to work from my home. No office required. No expensive ads needed. I just had to establish relationships with criminal defense attorneys and show them I could do a better job—that I could outperform any male bail agent!

Next up ... every company has to have a name. I grabbed a yellow notepad and started jotting down ideas. I thought that the company should have my name since the focus would be to provide my personal touch. I scribbled down *Sophie's Bail Bonds*. Then I immediately crossed it out. *Nobody's going to call 'Sophie's Bail Bonds*. I scribbled another … *Chickie's Bail Bonds.*

Perfect.

Next, I needed a tagline. I didn't have an office, and I didn't want anyone to come to my home. Somehow, some way, I had to turn that negative into a positive.

The more I thought about my business model, the more I liked it. I would make life easier for my clients by meeting them anywhere they wanted. They wouldn't have to schlep over to a bail-bond agent's office in a crummy part of town. I would go to them. All they had to do was call me on the telephone. I continued to scribble things down until I knew I had it.

Call Chickie… she comes to you.

Excitedly, I began banging around my home, scavenging for supplies. I didn't have much: a yellow notepad, some pens, a manual typewriter, and a telephone hanging on my kitchen wall. As I finished arranging everything, Fred wandered into the room. He had no idea what I had been up to. "Chickie," he asked, "why is the typewriter on the dining room table?"

"That's not the dining room table," I said with a wide smile.

"That's my office."

-3-

THIS COULD BE THE BEGINNING OF A BEAUTIFUL FRIENDSHIP

I was absolutely terrified. I was about to come face-to-face with my first criminal defense attorney. George Cameron convinced Beverly Hills lawyer Jeff Bear to meet me and now it was showtime. I had already decided on my professional outfit: a black pantsuit, black pumps, and conservative jewelry—emulating female attorneys in their courtroom attire, elegant and conservative. The "only-looks-expensive" briefcase completed my look.

I had always been known to overdress. When I went to the hospital for a minor surgical procedure many years ago, I wore a strapless dress in pink chintz fabric covered in roses. The doctor raised an eyebrow when he saw me and asked why I was all dressed up. I said, "Well, if I dress as though I'm going to a party, maybe someone will invite me to one." The doctor chuckled but it made sense to me.

Today would be the beginning of Chickie's Bail Bonds. All I had to do was to convince this prominent criminal defense attorney to refer his bail-bond business to this new kid on the block, a woman of my age with no retail experience! How likely was that?

When I knocked on Attorney Jeff Bear's office door, I wasn't sure if the sound I heard was my knuckles or my knees knocking! I tried not to look it, but felt so terribly nervous. I just hoped Jeff couldn't hear my heart pounding.

Jeff Bear answered the door himself—all six-foot-five inches of him—his dark long ponytail swinging behind him. His welcoming smile immediately put me at ease. I took a deep breath and launched into my spiel, explaining what I believed to be the advantage of working with a female bail-agent handling his clients instead of the gruff male-agent variety. Jeff listened, and although he seemed interested, he confessed he was a bit wary of working with a woman. He felt that men tended to be better suited for the role rather than "nice ladies" like me.

I told Jeff that's where he was mistaken. I explained that I didn't see defendants as "scum" the way most male agents did; that people deserved to be seen as more than the crime of which they were accused. "Nice ladies" like me had far more patience, empathy, and understanding than these so-called tough guys he was accustomed to working with. When Jeff stood up and extended his hand to me, I knew he was sold. My argument was sound—a woman bail agent would be far more empathetic than our male counterparts—and I had just established my first attorney relationship.

When Jeff began scribbling down names of several criminal defense attorney friends he was recommending me to, I was thrilled. Some of the lawyers said that they hadn't enjoyed working with male agents because of their gruff attitude and were willing to try working with a woman. A few still wouldn't budge no matter what I said, but it didn't matter. I had won over enough of these attorneys that Chickie's Bail Bonds was officially in business—and I was going to need more pantsuits.

On the phone, I had told her to look for the 50-year-old redhead dressed in black. My client looked exhausted, like she hadn't slept. That was how I knew it was her.

It was around 9 p.m. I was sitting in a booth at Dolores' Diner, a bran muffin and a decaf coffee on the table. This was going to be my first client, my first opportunity to prove myself. As my client approached, I sat up straight, very straight. *Here we go!*

I motioned for Debra to take a seat. She looked relieved to see me. "You know ... you aren't what I was expecting *at all*." This would become a common refrain in my years as a bail agent.

My first thought was to make sure I said all the right things and used the right bail-bond jargon. If she realized this was the first bond I had ever written, she might get angry and leave. I had to come across as a seasoned bail-bond agent. Calm, cool, and collected.

Debra explained that her son had been arrested and was locked up in the Los Angeles County Jail. "It's not the first time, either," she added, sounding thoroughly annoyed. Her son was paying the price of gang affiliation and Debra was at her wit's end. I expressed genuine sympathy for her situation and told her that I, too, had a son. This established a sense of understanding between us—a camaraderie.

As we sat together and drank coffee, Debra impressed me as an articulate, educated woman. My nervousness began to dissolve. It was as if we were two old friends chatting about our sons. She felt comforted by our conversation. In that moment I came to realize that there are no business relationships, only personal relationships. This wasn't a client talking about a defendant, but a mother talking about her son.

I assured Debra that I would soon have her son released and drove to downtown Los Angeles to post the two bonds. To "post a bond" means providing the jail with a surety insurance company's bail-bond form which has been executed by a licensed bail-bond agent indicating the arrestee's name, the charges, amount of the bail, and the date the defendant is to appear in court.

Debra's son required two $10,000 bonds because he was

wanted in two courts. As I filled out the paperwork, I made sure to follow George Cameron's instructions about filling out the "yellows," as they were called—small forms unique to Los Angeles County Jail.

A bail-bond agent's fee—or premium—is determined by the Department of Insurance at ten percent of the bond amount. After I had completed my first and second bonds, I received a fee of $2,000 in cash and Debra signed a deed of trust on her home, my guarantee that her son would make all of his court appearances. Debra was responsible for the two $10,000 bonds I had posted for her son's release. There was no way she would allow her son to leave town, leaving her responsible to pay the court $20,000.

Two-thousand dollars! That was my premium money; money I had earned by posting Debra's son's two bonds and being responsible for his appearance in court every time the court ordered him to.

TWO THOUSAND DOLLARS! I couldn't believe it! This was more money than I had ever seen at one time. It was absolutely wild! I remember thinking, *What should I do? What do I do with all this money?*

Before the internet, one of the ways to get your company's name out there was through flyers. With a minimal financial investment, I created a flyer to mail out to bail agents around the country. The flyer said:

> **Don't get out of bed tonight.**
> **Let Chickie do it and it'll be alright.**

Perhaps not the most articulate ad but it worked. No doubt our Chick logo, crashing through the jail bars, caught eyes.

Within a short time, I received a telephone call from a bail agent in Florida whose client was being held in local federal custody on the charge of drug dealing. As a new agent, all the bonds I had posted were in state court, but I wasn't going to let that get in the way. Within a few minutes, I had won this agent over and agreed to handle the case.

I drove to the Federal Correctional Institution on Terminal Island to meet with my defendant, Jeff Murray. The facility was on an actual island and struck me as the perfect place to house accused criminals who were awaiting their dates in federal court. Having the facility surrounded by water was a great deterrent to anyone considering trying to escape, plus there were a significant number of guards always making their presence known. That meant that it was going to be quite a drive, though.

In the days before GPS, and with my limited directional ability, I merely drove south in the general direction of Terminal Island to interview Jeff, hoping I would not get lost. I wondered why my client was housed such a distance from the downtown federal court where his case would be heard.

In a bit of a reverie, I thought of my great nephew Kevin Mitnick, who was held for almost five years in downtown Los Angeles federal correctional housing where Mitch and I, as licensed bail agents, could visit him regularly until the authorities became aware that Kevin was not entitled to bail visitation. He was being held without the possibility of bail. Great idea down the drain.

I was a frequent visitor when Kevin was brought before the court. I loved hearing the prosecutor declare that Kevin had not attempted to take one dime from anyone in all of his years of hacking, that it was the intellectual curiosity that drove him—the thrill of the challenge. I wondered what kind of thrills Jeff had been chasing.

Meeting Jeff Murray for the first time was very surprising. Knowing he was a drug dealer, I had visions of an older hardened criminal type, but Jeff was none of these things. He was tall, young, and handsome with a most engaging personality. And he was Jewish. I couldn't help thinking, *If he was in any other profession, I would have introduced him to my daughter!*

Jeff had been making quite a bit of money selling drugs and was living a luxurious lifestyle. He drove a brand-new sports car and dined at his favorite high-end Beverly Hills restaurant, The Palm, at least five nights a week.

In the 80s, The Palm was the storied steakhouse where all the movie stars and top models would schmooze—there was Tina Turner dancing on the bar and Evel Knievel parking his motorcycle inside the restaurant—a hotbed of Hollywood celebrities. And Jeff could be found there living like a star.

And now here he was, behind bars in a jail cell.

I liked Jeff immediately but that wasn't enough. I also confirmed that his parents were providing the collateral for his bond. If he should flee, they would be responsible to pay the court the full amount of his bail. I felt there was no way he would let that happen. I knew he would make all his required appearances and told him not to worry, that I would bail him out as soon as the court would allow.

Jeff's federal case meant that I would need to make an appearance in federal court, appear on the stand, take an oath to tell the truth, and give testimony. I felt honored to play such an important part in a court hearing.

In federal court, a "Nebbia hearing" is required where drugs are involved. It was my job to testify as to where the funds (the premium charged for the bond), and the collateral (usually real estate to guarantee the client's appearance) originated. Anything belonging to the defendant was a no-no. In Jeff's case, it was his mother who provided all we needed.

Waiting to testify in court, I felt like an actor about to take the stage before a large audience. I didn't have "lines," but I did know that if I messed up it could be the difference between Jeff getting out of jail or not.

I had always loved performing but it could be a nerve-wracking experience.

After Fred and I married, we joined Temple Shalom in West Covina, and I was offered the opportunity to participate in their drama group. I was thrilled to be in a play directed by Ricky Burkhart, first cousin to legendary comedian Don Rickles. I played the role of Dolly Levi in the play *The Matchmaker*, which was later adapted as the Broadway musical and feature film *Hello Dolly* with Barbra Streisand. I loved being on stage. I couldn't sing and I couldn't dance but I loved to act. The fact that I might not have any talent didn't really cross my mind.

I felt I was born to play the part of the smart and outspoken Dolly Levi. The word "can't" didn't exist in Dolly's vocabulary. And I was damn good at playing her. I remember how angry I was because Fred didn't bring a camera with him to the performance—and he always had a camera with him.

Years after my performance Fred would say, "Chickie, you have become Dolly Levi." And he was right. Even many years later I felt I was Dolly Levi. Maybe I still am.

I heard the loud banging of the gavel in the courtroom. The "play" had begun.

Hands sweating and heart pounding, I almost felt I was the one on trial when called to the witness stand. But as I sat down in front of the judge, the attorneys, and the rest of the courtroom, a sudden calm took over me.

I channeled my inner Dolly Levi. I wasn't wearing her elbow-length gloves or wide-brimmed silk hat, but I had her attitude, just as Dolly Levi with her chutzpa, convincing Mr. Vandergelder she had a beautiful young woman for him when all along she knew she would win him over for herself.

And then I was fine. More than fine. I confidently explained why Jeff should be released from jail, then I detailed the substantial collateral that had been offered to ensure his return. The court was convinced and Jeff was successfully bailed out.

I must have done well because after the proceedings, I was approached by Attorney Anna Ho, who said, "I like your style. Give me your card." Anna and I became business associates and good friends which continued even when it was appropriate to address her as "Your Honor."

Unfortunately, that wasn't the last time Jeff needed my services. In fact, I bailed him out several times. Our meetings were always bittersweet—it was nice to see him, but it meant he had gotten into trouble again. As much as I rooted for him to make good choices, he had fallen into a pattern.

I always felt it was a pity Jeff had chosen drugs as a way to make a living, especially when I could tell he had such potential.

One day Jeff called to tell me he was in custody again. "Don't worry, Jeff. I'll be right down!" I almost hung up the phone, but I could hear that he was still talking. "No, no, no, no! They got me for real, Chickie. I'm going to serve time. I may as well start now."

My heart sank. It felt like a part of me was in there with him. It had finally reached the point where I could no longer do anything to help him. Just devastating.

Jeff continued, "What's worse is I've got friends on the outside that owe me a lot of money and now I can't get any of it." Without really thinking about what that would mean, I offered to go and get Jeff's money for him—anything that could help. There was a long pause on the other end of the phone. "No, Chickie. That's okay."

After I hung up, it suddenly dawned on me that I had just offered to go pick up drug money. I could not believe that I had opened my big mouth! But I was right about Jeff, he was a good kid. He never would have put me at risk for anything—even for all of that money.

Ultimately Jeff was convicted and served two years in federal custody. It was time for him to pay his debt to society.

When I next heard from Jeff, years after his release, it was a phone call on my business line, and I thoroughly expected he would need me to post another bond for him. But the first words out of his mouth were, "Hey, Chickie. Guess what? I'm not a drug dealer anymore." Jeff explained that he had become friendly with the institution's rabbi who had helped change his attitude and guided him to a better way of life.

Jeff had opened a small trucking company, met a nice girl, settled down, and had a couple of kids. He was just a regular Joe earning a modest living. He wasn't making anywhere close to the money he did by selling drugs, but he had completely straightened his life out.

Well, this was music to my ears! I told Jeff how incredibly proud I was of him and that I wanted to do something in honor of his transformation. There was one gift that made perfect sense. I treated him to dinner at his favorite restaurant, The Palm.

It was great to see him. Still handsome as ever and finally doing something positive in his life. As soon as our waiter brought us our wine, I raised my glass and made a toast, "Here's to being my success story and staying one!" We clinked glasses. It was a very special moment.

While saying our goodbyes, Jeff expressed how grateful he was for the dinner. Jeff said he couldn't believe that he used to eat there five nights a week. He was shocked that I, his former bail-bond agent, had spent this kind of money on him.

Dolly Levi was right when she compared money to manure—it's the spreading around that makes it worth something.

NEVER JUDGE A BOOK BY ITS COVER

My phone was not ringing and the silence was deafening. Chickie's Bail Bonds had been up and running for a few months, and although I had had some success, I was discovering that the business of bail was cyclical. One week I would be busy and the next, nothing. No rhyme or reason. It could drive you nuts! There were days when I stared at the phone for hours, almost willing it to ring. Every now and then Fred would catch me looking at the phone and say, "Why don't you get a real job?" It wasn't that Fred didn't want me to succeed in business, it was just so foreign to him that I would start my own company. Fred was a good man who went to work to support us every day, in spite of adversity. As an engineer for the LA County Road Department, he had a completely different mentality. You go to work, you come back, that's it. His wife goes to work, she comes back, that's it. Starting a business would be the last thing in the world Fred would even consider. It was not that he thought of me as being particularly capable or incapable. He just thought of me as his wife.

Although I couldn't deny the negative thoughts that crept up at times like this, I felt compelled to push through Fred's skepticism. Each time I heard him say, "Get a real job," I silently made a vow I would make him eat his words, that one day I would make enough money from Chickie's Bail Bonds to buy him the condominium of his dreams—a luxurious condo on a golf course—then he would see!

Finally—the phone rang. I grabbed it quickly, smoothing down my hair to make myself presentable, even though it was only a phone call.

I cleared my throat.

"This is Chickie. May I help you?"

I always made a point to be courteous as possible when I answered the phone. This was another way I could distance myself from the male agents who were known to answer phones with a rude "Yeah" or a gruff voice would loudly bark out "BAIL BONDS!" Why would you do that? Why would you offend people before they even start talking to you?

The man on the phone introduced himself as George Smith. George confidently told me he was the president of a real estate company and that one of his employees had recently been arrested. George asked me to post a $5,000 bond. That would be five hundred dollars for me and a great start to the week!

I agreed to meet Mr. Smith at one of his investment properties—a condominium development in a nice, suburban neighborhood. He said his company owned six of the units and he had been living in one of them.

Pulling into the condominium parking lot, I admired how manicured the lawns were, the trees perfectly pruned, surrounded by colorful flower bushes.

An impeccably dressed gentleman greeted me with a smile at the condo's front door. He repeated his telephone bravado reminding me that this condo was only one of the six his company owned. Mr. Smith was wearing a magnificent black silk suit with a white tie and matching monogrammed hanky in his pocket. "George Smith," he said as he handed me a fancy business card with the company name "Smith & Associates" engraved in gold. I noted that the office address was a very nice area on Wilshire Boulevard in Beverly Hills. Clearly, this man was doing quite well for himself.

The condo had shiny wood floors with cream-on-cream walls, quite popular in the 80s. Brass wall sconces accented the room, and two tall Ficus plants surrounded the bay window. An interesting look, although not my taste. George invited me to have a seat on one of the grey tweed couches. I looked up and admired the beautiful glass chandelier that twinkled above us, like a million little stars.

I commented on how lovely his home was and asked if he was the one who had done the decorating. "Oh no," he laughed, "my wife did. She stepped out to the market for a few things. She'll be back shortly."

After we had exchanged more small talk, Mr. Smith signed the bail bond agreement which guaranteed that his employee, Daniel Shrieve, would appear in court. Then he signed the deed of trust form whereby he agreed to encumber his property as security against the bail amount.

His wife walked in, lugging two large bags of groceries, making her way slowly toward the kitchen. She was very pregnant. I remember thinking it strange that her husband didn't greet her with a kiss or offer any help, but knew it wasn't my place to say anything. There's more to marriage than chivalry and romance. What Fred and I had wasn't exactly what I would call romantic. It was more of a partnership. Everyone's relationship is different.

I drove away with my $500 premium safely tucked in my briefcase along with the necessary paperwork. I was impressed with Mr. Smith and had no doubt that his employee would make the required court appearances. Sure enough, he did. The court exonerated his bond, the matter was resolved, and everyone was happy. But it didn't end there.

A few weeks later I received a surprising phone call. "Chickie, it's George Smith. Do you remember me?"

"Of course I remember you!" I was sincere. Who could forget the man in the black silk suit?

George sounded upset. He told me he was being held in custody in Las Vegas. He insisted the arrest was a big mistake, that his identification had been used in a felonious property acquisition. Mr. Smith's voice broke as he pleaded with me to have him released as soon as possible so he could meet with his attorneys to straighten the whole thing out. "Chickie," he said, "you cannot imagine what I am going through, having my good name dragged through the mud!"

I understood. There was absolutely no reason for me not to trust him. I had seen George's luxury condo, his fancy business card, and his pregnant wife. I didn't hesitate to come to his aid. When you bail someone out of jail it is necessary to obtain as much information as you can, but not in this instance. I had already gotten a glimpse into George's life, so I wasn't worried at all.

A bail bond always comes with risk. The only time you can get hurt is when a defendant does not show up for court—then the bail bond agent becomes financially responsible for the full bail amount. In the bail industry this is known as a forfeiture. The deadly other F word.

In order to protect oneself, the agent must establish that the defendant has a job, family, and ties to the community, making it unlikely the defendant would flee.

George Smith had already been qualified; I had no reason to inquire further.

I was able to reach a reputable bail agent in Las Vegas to act on my behalf, posting the $10,000 bail. Mr. Smith assured me that he planned to return to LA the following day, at which time he would promptly pay my premium of $1,000 and sign the necessary paperwork, including the deed of trust on his condo to cover the $10,000 bond.

When I didn't hear from him the next day I didn't bat an eye. Things happen. People get delayed. Why should I suspect something was going awry? A successful family man in his position was a mover and a shaker. He was likely overloaded with important business deals.

A few days had passed when I finally heard from Mr. Smith.

This time he was even more distraught than when we had last spoken. He apologized for not contacting me sooner but said that something awful had happened. His voice cracked as he told me that his pregnant wife had been in a terrible automobile accident and was in the hospital. I was very concerned for his wife and their unborn baby. "There's no rush," I assured him. "Family is always top priority."

Over the next week we spoke almost every day while he was with his wife at the hospital. He would update me on his wife's progress but said that he wouldn't be able to meet with me until she and their unborn baby were out of the woods. His voice broke with the emotion of having his wife and unborn baby in such dire straits. Again, I understood.

Finally, the good news came. "My wife is coming home from the hospital today, Chickie!" George told me excitedly over the phone. "I'll see you next week to take care of everything!"

And then the phone calls stopped.

I tried calling George several times and left messages on his answering machine. No response. He still hadn't paid me the $1,000 for my services or signed any paperwork to guarantee the $10,000 bond.

Several more days passed and still no answer. A sinking feeling started to develop in the pit of my stomach. *Had I just been duped? Was this going to be my first forfeiture?*

A forfeiture is what gets you in the heart. It's a knife. A betrayal.

Impossible! The man was well off, had a nice condominium, and a pregnant wife who was just in the hospital. And he wore a black silk suit! There was no way this guy would skip out on me. Unless...

Unless it was all a lie.

I began pacing the floor, thinking about every single interaction I had with Mr. Smith. Those lies were going to cost me $10,000. The more I thought about it, the more foolish I felt. All those wasted days, kept on the hook, letting myself be dragged along.

The truth is that all bail agents have forfeitures. At some point it's going to happen. It's a known fact. I just never thought it would happen to me. *Not me!*

It was so hard to accept that Mr. Silk Suit was anything other than what he presented himself to be. I felt so foolish that I was taken in and wasted all those days. And where was I going to come up with $10,000?! That money would eat into my income from Chickie's Bail Bonds. That was a lot of money back then—that's a lot of money now! I could only imagine what Fred would think. I wanted him to believe that I could be a success. Now look at what happened.

To me, writing bail was something very personal. George Smith and I had spoken every day while he was at the hospital. I was patient, kind, and understanding, just as I was with all of my clients. I was good to him; therefore, he would be good to me. *Wouldn't he?*

I needed help. If George Smith had skipped town I would need to find him. I had no idea how to track somebody down, nor did I have the time for it. Not to mention I had to have Fred's dinner on the table by 6 p.m. There was only one thing left to do.

I dialed George Cameron's number.

George had been down this road before and calmly said that it was time for me to hire a bounty hunter.

People often think that a bail bond agent is the same as a bounty hunter, but that's not true. A bounty hunter is an entirely different breed. They're the ones who track down defendants who jump bail. They're also known as private investigators, bail enforcement agents, or fugitive recovery agents. Not only do they have to know all the ins and outs of investigative work, they have to be ready to encounter potentially dangerous situations.

The only time a bounty hunter makes money is if they find the person. It's a crapshoot. You could knock yourself out for six months, never find the guy, and not make a cent. When George told me this, I remember thinking it was the stupidest thing I'd ever heard. Then I realized that bounty hunters weren't in it for the money. They were in it for the thrill of the hunt.

Al Schlagle became my first bounty hunter. When we spoke on the phone, I didn't quite know what to make of him. We arranged to meet at Dolores's Diner later in the day. It was an ideal location, just fifteen minutes from my Santa Monica home.

Everyone at Dolores's knew me by name. They knew I took my coffee decaf with a splash of steamed milk and no sugar. And always a bran muffin. I loved a good bran muffin. I've since learned, however, there's a lot of calories in bran muffins, so that kind of blows the whole healthy thing.

With three pay phones almost within reach of my barstool, Dolores's was the perfect mobile office for me. I used one phone for outgoing calls and one for incoming, leaving the third phone free for other customers' use. Armed with my trusty yellow notepad, Chickie's Bail Bonds was fully mobile!

A waitress led a rugged-looking man through the crowded restaurant. I had talked to Al Schlagle on the phone but had no idea what to expect and yet he was somehow exactly what I had imagined. It made sense that someone whose occupation is finding those who do not want to be found would appear as he did—nondescript—absolutely fitting the bill. His eyes darted around the restaurant, missing nothing.

As Al moved toward me, I saw he walked with a limp, some affliction, most likely MS. But apparently it didn't affect his reputation as being the best in the business. His wrinkled blue plaid shirt, half-tucked into his light-colored khakis, gave the impression he had just rolled out of bed.

Al got right to work. No small talk. He quickly rifled through my paperwork—barely saying a word to me as I told him about my situation. He stopped shuffling briefly and told me he could help me avoid paying $10,000 to the Las Vegas court and get my $1,000 premium. Then he went back to silently shuffling through papers.

I hope this guy knows what he's doing.

Suddenly, Al clapped his hands to indicate he was done. "Come on. Let's go!"

Before I had a chance to grab my bran muffin, Al was headed out the door. I grabbed my briefcase and ran after him. He was surprisingly fast.

When I finally caught up to him, all out of breath, I managed to gasp out, "Where are we going?"

"To the condo, of course," he said, starting up the car. "Maybe we can catch him before he takes off."

I eyeballed this strange man in his strange car which looked very much like a police vehicle—an old model brown Impala. I didn't know if his idea was good or not, but I tumbled into the passenger seat.

As we drove onto George Smith's property I couldn't believe my eyes. The beautifully manicured lawn I remembered was now covered with trash cans, litter, and cardboard boxes. We approached the front door of George's condo. All the lights were off. I tried ringing the doorbell while Al went right to pounding his fists on the door. *BAM BAM BAM.*

"Anybody home?" Al yelled out. No answer.

Al cocked his head to one side and quickly scanned the area. His eyes darted up and down and around like a hawk until he found what he was looking for. "Window," he said.

Sure enough there was an open window on the second floor of the condo. I was about to ask Al how we would get up there, but he was already halfway up a tree next to the window. I watched in disbelief as he slid off a tree branch, into the open window, and disappeared.

I looked around nervously, making sure nobody was watching. I wasn't one hundred percent sure of the legality of what Al was doing but he was the professional.

Suddenly the front door flung open from the inside. Al stood there, shaking his head. "He's gone."

Incredulous, I followed Al into the condo. The inside was completely empty—no luxury furniture, no brass wall sconces, and trash strewn everywhere. George had taken everything including the beautiful glass chandelier. In its place was a gaping hole with wires jutting out.

Al tore through every box and every carton in the condo. He scrutinized every scrap of paper and piece of trash he could find. He was like a machine. "Here … hold this." Al handed me a slip of paper as he continued to dig. "And this."

Phone bills, receipts, faxes. To the untrained eye it was just junk, but Al was determined to find the trail that would help us locate the elusive George Smith.

"Garbage bin," I heard Al mutter as he hurried out the front door.

I followed behind, just in time to see him climb into the dumpster. My professional future and self-respect were in the hands of this Al Schlagle, a bounty hunter who was rummaging through the garbage.

Being a wife and mother, I reflexively winced that his light pants were going to get all stained. *He's going to ruin those khakis—his wife is going to have to scrub those pants!*

"You just missed him!" a nearby voice yelled out. "His truck pulled out less than an hour ago." It was a female neighbor walking her dog. "Was he with his wife?" I asked. The woman gave me a blank stare. "Wife?"

I described the pregnant woman I had seen before, and the neighbor said she had never seen anyone matching that description. The neighbor then went on to say that George Smith didn't own six condos in the development. She almost laughed when I asked. George Smith didn't even own "his" condo. He had only been renting it.

I was losing hope. I felt my bail-bond agent skills were in serious question. It was almost inevitable that this would be my first forfeiture. Every aspect of George's life seemed to be a fabrication. I'll bet he didn't even own that silk suit.

Then it occurred to me that I still had the engraved business card for Smith and Company with the fancy address on Wilshire Boulevard.

Al and I got back into his Chrysler and sped off, knowing in my heart of hearts how unlikely it was that Mr. Smith would be there. Al explained that even if Mr. Smith wasn't at the office, there still could be more clues with which to track him down. Al still had the faint smell of garbage on him. I discreetly rolled down the window.

It took about 20 minutes for us to arrive at the address on the business card. Instead of one of the majestic office buildings that lined Wilshire Boulevard as I had expected, the address on the card took us to a vacant parking lot. I lowered my head in defeat. There were no clues to be found here. Yet Al was unfazed.

Driving back to Dolores's, Al's rattletrap car weaving in and out of traffic, I was filled with shame. It was not that forfeitures were unheard of in my business, quite the contrary. But to think how I was so foolish to let this drag on for so long.

After we arrived at Delores's, Al explained that he had uncovered enough bits and pieces of information to form a decent picture of where the fugitive might be headed. He wouldn't tell me anything more.

My financial fate was in Al's hands. I had done my part of the bounty hunting, and it was up to him to finish the job. I had no idea how that would work. *How can you find someone who doesn't want to be found?*

The next few weeks were hell for me as the calendar counted down to the deadline for George Smith's initial court appearance. I was not surprised to learn that the defendant was a no-show. It was official. I had my first forfeiture.

From that point, I had 180 days to find my defendant, or I would have to pay the court the $10,000 that was due. Al Schlagle was still on the hunt.

I didn't want to bother Al, but I couldn't resist calling him regularly to check in. After all, I had $10,000 on the line! He said the same thing whenever we talked. "These things take time,

Chickie." Easy enough for him to say. It was my money and credibility at risk! I still hadn't figured out how I would cover the $10,000 or explain this whole situation to Fred.

Another 10 weeks went by without a shred of news about the whereabouts of Mr. Smith. "These things take time, Chickie," he repeated. *Okay, but how much time?* It was so nerve-wracking, I could barely sleep a wink.

With less than two months left before the deadline, I was sitting on my gray swivel stool at Dolores's when I received the call. It was Al Schlagle calling me for once.

As I cradled the phone to my ear, I heard Al say the magic words I had been dying to hear. "George Smith has been taken into custody in Las Vegas. We did it!"

"Damn straight we did!" I practically yelled into the phone.

I was overcome with relief! Curious, I asked Al how he managed to crack the case, but as with most investigators, Al kept tight-lipped about his methods. This was fine with me. All that mattered was that Mr. Smith would face all of the charges levied against him and I was off the hook for the $10,000 bond I had posted. I had to pay Al for his service, but that was peanuts.

My first forfeiture had to happen at some point and I was glad to have it out of the way with only minimal damage to my bank account and self-esteem. I had learned an invaluable lesson from this experience: Never judge a prospective client by a gold embossed business card, a beautiful condo, or a silk suit.

Everyone has a "first" that ranks high on their list of momentous events. A first kiss, a first date, the birth of a first child. For a bail-bond agent there is an entirely different range of memorable "firsts" that are impossible to forget: the first bond written, the first premium received and, inevitably, the first forfeiture.

That night as Fred and I enjoyed the delicious chicken pot pie I had made for dinner, I thought about how close I had come to having to fork over $10,000 of my hard-earned money. I had been on pins and needles for months. So many sleepless nights and stressful days wondering…

I felt as though a heavy weight had been lifted off my shoulders. Al Schlagle, my first bounty hunter, had succeeded in capturing my fraudulent fugitive. The manhunt was over.

"How was your day?" Fred asked me, in between bites.

"Oh, you know. Just another day at work."

-5-

A SURPRISING SLANT, A MILLION DOLLARS

I almost dropped the phone!

A bail agent was calling to ask if I would consider splitting a one-million-dollar bond with him. His insurance company would not let him write that large a bond. I, however, was in a very unique position. Although still a "green" agent, I had been involved with the bail industry in corporate roles for many years. With my stalwart reputation, Mike presumed my insurer would allow me to write a bond of this size and he was right!

Splitting the premium with Mike, my cut would be $50,000—a tasty sum indeed! Some bail agents never get the chance to write a bond for $100,000, let alone one for a million dollars. So, this was a very big deal.

For that much money I couldn't help but wonder what kind of crime this could possibly be. Mike told me that his client's wife, Kimi Yamashiro, was being held in custody at the Los Angeles County Jail and that she had been arrested on charges of bribery. One million dollars was such an exorbitant amount of money. My interest was piqued.

I agreed to meet Mr. Yamashiro at a coffee shop near his Los Angeles home. He was a Japanese gentleman of about 70 years of age. He had a dignified air about him with a facial expression that was quite stoic.

If I was going simply on appearances, I would have assumed that he was quite well-off, but I had learned my lesson with Mr. Smith that appearances can be deceiving. This time the stakes were a lot higher. 100 times higher, to be exact. If this defendant skipped town as Mr. Smith had, I would be on the hook for an astronomical amount of money. There was simply no room for mistakes.

Mike Brown had already done some preliminary information gathering but I needed to find out everything I could about Mr. Yamashiro and his wife myself. I took my yellow notepad out of my briefcase and began asking questions. Though terse, Mr. Yamashiro provided me with his full name and residential address as well as verifying his relationship to the defendant. It was all pretty straightforward. But the most important information I needed was to confirm that Mr. Yamashiro had enough property to cover the collateral on a million-dollar bond. As soon as I began inquiring about his finances he immediately clammed up.

"That's a private matter," he said.

Not a great start, I mused.

Then I asked him about what kind of assets he had.

"That's a private matter."

It was like pulling teeth. After several more answers like that I put my notepad down. If Mr. Yamashiro wouldn't communicate with me, then I needed to change my strategy. I found that every situation demands a different persona and you have to make adjustments when necessary. It doesn't mean being phony or false. You want to present yourself in a way that you will be best received.

Growing up in Boyle Heights, I was used to a melting pot of cultures. Although the neighborhood was primarily Jewish, my classes in school had students who were Mexican, Black, Japanese, and a smattering of Russians. Being around such ethnic diversity helped me understand people and appreciate our similarities and differences. I felt comfortable taking on clients of every ethnicity and culture.

It had been my experience that East Asians placed a lot of value on privacy. They believed it very important to keep up appearances, sometimes referred to as "saving face," so as to not bring negative attention to the family.

I don't imagine that anyone, even in Mr. Yamashiro's closest circle, had any idea that Mrs. Yamashiro had been arrested. I surmised that he must have felt somewhat ashamed and was putting up walls to protect himself. And it was up to me to break them down.

This was a very serious man, so I put on the most serious face I could. "Mr. Yamashiro, I'm about to loan you a million dollars. Any question I ask, you have to answer, because I have to feel confident with whom I am dealing."

He was keeping everything close to the vest and clearly didn't want to give out information to just anyone. He had to know me first before he was willing to reveal the details that I needed to be able to secure his wife's release. I had to earn this man's trust fairly quickly.

I looked him in the eye and assured him that I would do everything in my power to protect him and his wife's privacy. I've always considered that an important part of my work. Then I went on to say, "I want you to know that I am on your side and I'm going to get your wife out as soon as possible. But in order to help you, I need you to help me."

Our exchange up until this point had all been fairly impersonal, so I decided to ask him about his family to see if that would loosen him up. I wanted him to see that we were both human beings. The serious look on his face softened and he told me that he and his wife had moved to Los Angeles from Japan less than two years ago with their three grown children. Finally, we were making some progress! I told him that I had two grown children of my own and showed him photos of my daughter Karen and my son Mitch that I kept in my wallet.

With that common ground established between us, I pressed on and asked him to tell me about what happened with his wife's arrest. Mr. Yamashiro confided in me that this was just a business deal that had fallen through. He and his wife had purchased vacant land in

Culver City on which to build a motel and proceeded to plan the construction. During the process, their architect surprised them with some new information: They would need the city's approval in order to break ground.

To their dismay, the Culver City Planning Commission denied their request, citing that the area was not suitable for that type of establishment due to its close proximity to an elementary school. The couple then took their request to the Culver City Council but unfortunately, the end result was the same: Request denied.

Refusing to give up, they decided that their next step would be to contact a city councilman directly. In that Mrs. Yamashiro's command of English was much better than her husband's, she was the one who called the office of Herbert Allen, a Culver City councilman, and arranged to see him.

Mrs. Yamashiro met with the councilman in his office a few days later. She reminded him of the recent motel development plans that had been denied and offered to pay him a generous amount of cash in exchange for his agreement to coax the city council into approving the request.

Well, that certainly sounded like bribery to me.

Mr. Allen told Mrs. Yamashiro that he would have to think about her offer and get back to her. Again, the Yamashiros were hopeful that their plans would be moving forward.

The following week, Mr. Allen called and arranged to meet with Mrs. Yamashiro at his office. During their meeting, they went over the particulars of the deal once more where she explicitly stated she would give him cash for help influencing the city council.

Seconds later Mrs. Yamashiro was being handcuffed by the police. It was a set up. Mr. Allen had been wearing a wire. He had gone to the mayor, and it was agreed that this "offer" had to be brought to the attention of law enforcement. Attempting to bribe an elected official was a serious charge.

Mr. Yamashiro was adamant that his wife was innocent. Despite his cool demeanor, I could sense that he was deeply alarmed by his wife's incarceration. I thought perhaps something was getting lost in translation. How could he possibly think his wife was innocent?

Mr. Yamashiro informed me that what we consider bribery in the United States is simply the norm in Japan and that local officials don't just take bribes … they expect them!

I couldn't believe it! It sounded as if it was just a misunderstanding resulting from cultural differences. One big, expensive misunderstanding. Even though what is considered right in one place and time, may be wrong in another. However, the law is still the law in the United States.

And there was still the matter of Mr. Yamashiro's collateral.

In the course of our conversation, I had gained his trust enough for him to eventually feel comfortable in revealing what his personal holdings were. He provided me with sufficient information to justify my taking such a huge risk.

With all of the details now sorted out, I told him that once he paid the $100,000 premium for the one-million-dollar bond, I could get his wife released quickly. Most bail agents would have left it at that. Get the huge premium payment and get out.

However, I chose to explain that since it was a Friday, Mrs. Yamashiro's bail had been set at a very high one million dollars. I told Mr. Yamashiro that if his wife remained in custody over the weekend, her million-dollar bail would be reduced to $100,000 when she appeared in court on Monday; that the $100,000 premium for the million-dollar bond if posted on Friday would be only $10,000 on Monday for the posting of the $100,000 bond.

In this situation, almost every person would have allowed their spouse to stay in custody over the weekend. In my opinion a weekend was practically nothing. A short stint. The savings would be a great deal.

"No. I want my wife out now."

That was it. No hesitation. No conversation. He refused to allow his beloved wife to spend one more minute in custody than was absolutely necessary.

I remember thinking that if I had been in this situation, I would insist that Fred have me stay in jail over the weekend. Fred would have agreed with me. We were on the same page about saving money.

A weekend apart wasn't a big deal. After all, Fred and I were apart for the entire first year of our marriage.

At the age of 17 and just ten days out of high school, a hundred guests danced at my wedding. It was a beautiful, although hastily planned ceremony, and the circumstances behind it were far from romantic. My childhood friend Lorraine, whom I had known since nursery school, was my maid of honor.

My mother basically manipulated Fred into marrying me, "If you do not marry Chickie before you leave for Korea, I will see to it she is not waiting for you when you return."

Harsh as it may seem, I know my mother's intentions were good. She used to tell me and my sister that the worst thing in life was to be alone. Sadly, this had become her destiny after divorcing my father and she felt that it was better to be with somebody than nobody. Even if that somebody wasn't the love of your life.

Fred and I had started dating when I was in high school although he was a full four years older than me.

As an impressionable young girl, I believed in romance like I saw it on the big screen every Saturday afternoon. My girlfriends had success with boys where I did not and I was jealous. I wanted a boyfriend too. My mother was intent on my settling down with a nice Jewish boy. She was so afraid that I would marry a non-Jew. Fred had all the qualifications—he was bright, ambitious, tall, good looking, and Jewish.

When the Korean War started, Fred joined the Army Corps of

Engineers to avoid being drafted into the infantry. He was stationed at Ft. Belvoir, Virginia and wrote to me daily, although sometimes he was so exhausted he could only write the words "I love you." This was more than enough for me. I felt like my heart would burst. I was in love and it was wonderful!

When Fred had his first 10-day leave, he came home and surprised me with a ring. I enthusiastically said yes, but neither of us had any idea when we would actually get married. We were young and had lots of time. Or so we thought.

Just one month later, Fred received the bad news that he was being sent to Korea for a year to build airstrips. I was crushed. He was given another 10-day leave and once again we were reunited. Although it was wonderful to see him, there was this feeling of not knowing if I would ever see him again after he sailed away. That's when my mother decided to take matters into her own hands.

My mother had been deathly ill for a long time, and she wasn't sure that she would survive. She couldn't bear the thought of leaving me on my own, which is why she had threatened Fred.

Fred knew it was not a good idea to marry, have sex for the first time, and then disappear for a year. However, believing my mother's threat, he agreed. He really loved me and didn't want to risk losing me. Less than a week later one hundred friends danced at our wedding!

I traveled to Ft. Ord so that I could be with Fred until he shipped out. Sadly, our time together was cut short when my sister called to say the ambulance was on its way to take my mother to the hospital. I was on the next plane home.

Our relationship flourished via the U.S. mail. While in Korea, Fred wrote to me every day, reporting on his daily activities. They were all fairly matter of fact, but it was always a thrill to receive them. I remember one was just a messy scribble that said, "Too drunk to write!" It wasn't poetry but it was still lovely to hear from him.

Frequently his letters arrived out of order. One day I received a very upsetting one in which he reported that he was in the hospital and the sitz baths "seemed to be helpful." I was terribly worried, to say the least. I had no idea what had happened to him. All I knew was that a sitz bath was a warm, shallow bath that cleanses your backside region. I feared that perhaps his butt had gotten blown off!

The next day I received the letter he'd written earlier in which he explained that he was going into the hospital to be treated for a rectal abscess. Painful, to be sure, but hardly as serious as what I had envisioned. Thankfully his butt was still intact.

When Fred returned from overseas, at last I found myself in his arms—a moment I had been longing for an entire year. It was, however, very peculiar. After 365 days this skinny man with his shaved head was a total stranger. He even smelled different. While in Korea, he'd taken up smoking and now he chewed Juicy Fruit gum to cover his breath. The combination of odors was awful, like a pineapple ashtray. But the important thing was that he was home. And we were finally starting our new life together.

Finding an apartment in our price range was a challenge. The government was paying Fred $200 a month to finish his college education. We found a two-bedroom apartment in City Terrace, in the hills above East Los Angeles, at $60 a month. But we had the additional expense of a beautiful surprise—our daughter Karen was born nine months and one day after Fred's ship landed. Fortunately, I had put aside every penny I earned the year he was in Korea, so we were able to furnish our apartment and buy a 1948 Chevy for cash.

Fred attended East Los Angeles Jr. College in the daytime and studied at night, the bright lamp on our bedroom desk helping him to stay awake while I slept in our double bed just feet away.

One night I was awoken from a sound sleep by loud banging on our front door. By the time I got there Fred had opened the door to a bruised and bleeding naked hysterical young woman whom he wrapped in a blanket. Fred had gently placed her on our living room couch. We offered to call the police, but she said no and called her brother to come and pick her up; she said he would handle it. While we waited, she told us her horrible story.

She, Alvira, an attractive college student, was walking in downtown Los Angeles on her way to meet her boyfriend when a car with a pleasant looking young man pulled up beside her. He told Alvira he knew her—that they shared a class at the local college. She was hesitant, but he convinced her that he would drive her to meet her boyfriend and she got in the car. Within moments, the car was filled with his friends; three in the backseat and one in the front, rudely pushing Alvira into the driver. She begged to be let out of the car but to no avail. The driver drove from downtown Los Angeles to east LA and up into the hills of City Terrace going around and around the steep hills while his buddies drank from the bottle they passed between them, laughing and joking about the events yet to come. Although she remembered cruising into the hills, she had no idea where she was.

When the car finally stopped, Alvira was dragged, stripped, sexually assaulted, and beaten by the five men. She passed out from the assault and revived to find herself alone, naked and bleeding in a strange rural area with no sign of her clothing. Half hysterical, she dragged herself to the road and began walking, hoping to find a house with a light on where she might find refuge. Fortunately, she eventually saw Fred's study lamp.

When Alvira's brother arrived, he thanked us for our kindness, although he was clearly much more concerned with his sister's terrible condition. We never heard from them again, and doubted they wanted to be reminded of that night.

This story has haunted me for over seventy years; how an innocent mistake almost cost a young woman her life.

Mr. Yamashiro's decision to pay the extra $90,000 to get his wife out of jail was staggering, to say the least. From a financial standpoint it was certainly a boon for my business, but I couldn't stop thinking, *Was this chivalry or an attempt to avoid losing face?*

I posted the one-million-dollar bond that night and Mrs. Yamashiro was released a couple of hours later. I watched with delight as Mr. and Mrs. Yamashiro embraced. Although still reserved, a smile slowly crept across Mr. Yamashiro's face. They looked tenderly into each other's eyes—clearly in love. No words needed.

I concluded that this was indeed an act of chivalry. This was romance. Like the kind I used to see on the big screen every Saturday afternoon. He was protecting his love from spending any time in jail where harm might come to her. Even if the harm was only to her pride.

The horrible ordeal of incarceration may have been over, but the Yamashiros' involvement with the American criminal justice system was only just beginning. Wisely, the couple hired a well-respected Japanese criminal defense attorney who was able to guide them through the mountain of differences between American and Japanese laws and customs.

As I expected, Mrs. Yamashiro made all of her court appearances with her devoted husband supporting her nearby in the courtroom. I sat there watching, hoping for the best. My gut feeling was that they had a good chance to get out of any serious trouble, but the criminal justice system is full of surprises, and nothing can be taken for granted.

The court was shown that there was no intent to commit wrongdoing. Kimi Yamashiro had merely been acting in accordance with the norms of her upbringing. Ultimately the charges were dismissed upon the payment of a nominal fine and her promise not to repeat the offense in the future.

After the trial I waited outside. I wanted to congratulate them and wish them luck with their future, but they had left without a word—returning to their private lives.

For me, part of this business involves going through all sorts of emotions with clients. Up and down through grief to elation, regret to redemption. And then it's all over. Sometimes you make a lifetime friend and sometimes you go from a confidante to a mere acquaintance. Like blowing out a candle. Poof. Gone.

I never heard from the Yamashiros again. But I had helped them on their way to a new life in America.

And to me, that was enough.

-6-

THE COP AND THE CON ARTIST

Once a con man, always a con man.

The term "con man" is short for confidence man—a beguiling swindler who works by gaining the confidence of the unknowing victim they are about to swindle.

When a person starts down that road, I've learned that they rarely come back. Deception almost becomes embedded in their DNA. Fallacies and betrayal are the status quo, all done under the cloak of irresistible charm. And anyone can fall prey to the con man's trickery—even a cop.

"There's a guy in jail with me who's going to cover my bail," Jason told me over the phone.

This was a new one. Usually when someone is bailed out of jail it's by family or friends, sometimes the odd work colleague or ex-girlfriend—people who have known the defendant for some time and feel comfortable taking on the financial obligation. But I had never heard of a cellmate offering to do it.

I didn't know exactly how Jason Westmorland had managed to convince this random stranger to pay for his bail bond but the one thing I did know was that Jason Westmorland was trouble.

The first time I dealt with Jason was when he was just 18 years old. The year was 1987 and he had been picked up for joyriding—taking a vehicle that belongs to someone else for a ride with no particular goal other than the thrill of doing so. Jason

61

had developed a proclivity to joyriding, but it was the first time he had actually been caught.

I met with Jason's mother in the basement of Robinson's—an upscale department store in Beverly Hills that was popular in the 80s. There was a cute little coffee shop there, quaint and private, although I felt that their bran muffins were a bit on the dry side.

As with most mothers I dealt with, Peggy Westmorland immediately tried to justify her son's actions. "It's not his fault," she said in a soft-spoken voice. Jason's father had died when Jason was very young and she had raised him by herself. "He wouldn't be getting in trouble if his father was still alive," she said, wringing her hands.

Peggy was inconsolable that her son was behind bars. Her "baby boy," as she called him. She proudly showed me a recent photo of Jason. He looked like a real Southern California kid—skinny and tan, with wild sandy blond hair and a mischievous smile.

Peggy said she worked full time for the phone company, which surprised me since she seemed somewhat elderly and frail. In actuality, she was only in her 60s.

Joyriding was a misdemeanor offense, so the bail amount wasn't that much. Peggy skittishly handed me a pink slip. "For collateral," she said. "It's the title for my car."

This dear, sweet woman. She had seen one too many movies. People are often shown giving pink slips to their cars as collateral for any number of various transactions but that isn't how it works in my business.

Normally I would not take a pink slip as collateral for a bond as they're perfectly worthless. A pink slip isn't a car; it's a piece of paper. Peggy and her son could easily take a joyride together and drive my "collateral" all the way off to Minnesota and that would be the end of that.

When I saw the look of desperation in Peggy's eyes I decided to make an exception. Her son was so young and baby faced, I felt he would never betray his mother by not showing up to court. I gave her a receipt for the small premium amount on the bond, and I held onto her pink slip, promising to return it when Jason's case was over.

Jason and I briefly spoke on the phone after his release. I warned him about making his court appearances and to let us know of any change of address or phone number. He agreed to everything wholeheartedly.

"Absolutely, Chickie. Absolutely."

A considerable time later, Jason was convicted for his offense. He had, in fact, made all of his court appearances and didn't skip out. He even took the trouble to call me after court to let me know that he would be serving time and wanted to make sure his mother received her pink slip back. I assured him that I returned it, pleased that he was so concerned about his mother. I remember thinking, *What a good kid.*

Or perhaps he was just trying to give the impression that he was a good kid?

I didn't hear from Jason for several years. When it comes to my clients, I always hope they don't get arrested again, that they're flourishing and doing whatever they need to do to improve their lives. Unfortunately, that wasn't the case for Jason.

This time Jason had landed himself in the Los Angeles County Jail for much more serious crimes. And there I was again, meeting with Peggy Westmorland, who was explaining away her son's criminal behavior again. True to form, Jason had been conning his mother already. "He was set up," she insisted.

Peggy explained that her son was being charged with grand theft auto. The prosecutors alleged that Jason would find ads in the local newspaper for people selling their expensive luxury cars: Mercedes, BMWs, Jaguars, you name it.

Jason would then meet the people at their homes, convince them that he was a legitimate buyer, and that he would buy the car. "I just need to take it out for a quick spin first," he would say. He'd take it out for a quick spin all right. And he would never come back. From the sound of it, Jason had graduated to a full-fledged con man.

When determining the amount of bail, the judge sets the dollar amount by considering the crime as well as the circumstances. In this case, Jason was charged with multiple counts of grand theft auto and he had a prior conviction. The bail amount was set very high—$175,000. The court had determined he was definitely a flight risk.

This was a huge amount even in the 80s. It was doubtful that Jason's mother had enough pink slips to cover this collateral! Not to mention the ten percent premium on the bond. Jason certainly didn't have the necessary resources, so unless circumstances miraculously changed, he was going to remain in custody.

It didn't take Jason long to figure out a scheme. While in jail awaiting his trial, he was placed in a cell with Ray Ford—a cop with two decades of law enforcement experience who had been sentenced to life in prison for murder in the first degree. Ford's story was featured in the newspapers with headlines like, "Cop Gone Bad" and "Rogue Cop Commits Murder."

Con men like to trifle with people's emotions. They target people who are going through times of extreme life change. They also like to set a ticking clock; a limited time offer that persuades someone to act quickly—a very calculated psychological tactic.

As far as Jason was concerned, the cop was a sitting duck.

The most successful con artists hinge on desire. What can they offer their target that will make them abandon all rational thought for the promise of some fantasy? And the best way to discover someone's desires is to ask a lot of questions. All that Ray Ford had to do was talk.

It was a harrowing story. Ray's wife Lillian was a bus driver in Los Angeles who worked the evening shift. At about 11p.m. Lillian observed a lone male passenger sitting at the back of the bus. When she pulled the bus over to make her final scheduled stop for the night, the man remained seated. Lillian walked to the back of the bus and kindly asked the man to leave. He leapt up and viciously attacked her.

Lillian was beaten, sexually assaulted, and left for dead on the floor of the bus. Barely breathing, she managed to crawl to the front of the bus and radio for help. Emergency vehicles were on the scene within minutes and were able to save her.

But they couldn't save her husband. As soon as he saw Lillian in the hospital covered in bruises and clinging to life, it was like a switch went off. This was his loving wife of 15 years and the mother of his two children. He completely lost his mind. He swore that if he ever found the man that did this to his wife, he would kill him. And while she convalesced in the hospital, he started looking. During the day he continued to work for the police force, but he spent every night searching high and low for the man who had done this to his wife.

The police detectives had narrowed their suspects down to one man, but while they were attempting to gather sufficient evidence to arrest him, Ray Ford went out on his own, tracked the suspect down, and shot him square in the chest multiple times.

The man was pronounced dead at the scene and Ray was taken into custody charged with murder. Since the crime was premeditated Ray couldn't plead temporary insanity or self-defense. He was sentenced to life in prison, without the possibility of parole.

Ray had seen the newspaper stories about him and was devastated that he was painted in such a bad light, leaving out his motive: the brutal assault on his wife. It goes without saying that the press has a tendency to latch onto the most scandalous details in criminal cases. In Ray's situation, the fact that he was a cop who killed someone was all that they cared about.

With these slanted articles about him, along with the harsh sentencing for the crime, Ray felt that his legacy was completely irreparable. It hurt him that his wife and two children would be followed by this dark shadow for the rest of their lives.

"I'm not a bad guy," he told Jason in their jail cell. "I wish I could get the real story out."

Jason had found his angle. He told Ray he had connections in Hollywood and could get a movie made about this man's life that would tell everyone what really happened. Selling this kind of story to a studio would be a slam dunk, according to Jason.

The caveat? Ray would have to provide the collateral and pay the premium of $17,500 to get Jason released from jail.

When Ray mentioned that Lillian was driving an old beat-up car, Jason also said he had a new Cadillac he would give to Lillian as a gift. This was the cherry on the sundae—Ray did care very much about his wife.

It was hard to believe that a veteran cop would fall for Jason's empty promises, but Ray took the bait—hook, line, and sinker. Ray offered the title to his house.

This was all moving very fast and I was dubious of the whole setup. When I spoke to Ray over the phone, I tried to explain all of the ramifications of this commitment and told him to seriously think over what he was about to do. "You have a family to think about," I cautioned. "If Jason should take off and not make his court appearances, you and Lillian will lose your home."

Blinded by his ego, Ray wouldn't budge. "People need to know the truth!"

The next day I met with Ray's wife at their house—the house that he was gambling away. She was such a timid little thing. It looked as if she had recovered from her injuries, at least physically. Lillian couldn't have been more than 30 years old and was very petite, even diminutive.

I felt so awful for her, knowing the horrifying details of what she had gone through. And now with her husband in jail, his vigilante justice instantly made her a single mother.

All Lillian had left in the world was this house and she wanted to turn it over to me so that I could get her husband's cellmate—an unscrupulous con man—out of jail. It made absolutely no sense. I was angry with the cop and his ego. I was angry with Jason and his scheme.

Even from jail, Lillian's husband was still ruling the roost and his decision was final. She was simply trying to be the good wife. Her husband was resolute to have the world know his story—even if it meant that his family might lose the roof over their heads.

"Why are you doing this?" I asked Lilli.

"My husband says I have to."

It was a line I had heard many times before.

Of all the accusations made against my clients, the one for which we are most often called upon to post bail is known as 273.5 of the Los Angeles Penal Code: Spousal Abuse.

Rhonda Woodward's husband had assaulted her, and she was calling me to bail him out of jail. Again, he had beaten her up—and when he was released from jail, the beatings would continue. It was a vicious cycle.

"My husband says I have to get him out right now."

I had helped bail Rhonda's husband out several times before and each time a twinge of uneasiness would run through me. I never judge the accused but at a certain point "innocent until proven guilty" goes right out the window.

Like many abused women, Rhonda had no one else to turn to. These men break their spouses down bit by bit until they're completely demoralized and alienated from friends and family. The only person the wife has left is the very person who is abusing them. The wife is all alone.

With my friends and family, I give advice whether asked for or not. I'm sure my friends all hate it because I think I know everything, but sometimes, like now, I do.

"Leave him in there," I told Rhonda. "You don't have to do this."

Despite her husband being in jail, Rhonda was still emotionally being held captive. I spent over an hour on the phone with her, giving her permission not to get him out. I must have said it to her a hundred different ways.

She finally relented as if awakening from a dark spell. "Okay, Chickie. I'm going to do it. I'm going to leave him in there." She let out a deep sigh of relief, like a weight had been lifted from her shoulders. I was so proud of her. "Good for you, Rhonda. You're done with him."

After I hung up the phone, Fred said to me, "You need a couch. You're not a bail agent. You're a psychologist."

I still receive a Christmas card from Rhonda every year.

As wary of Jason Westmorland's sincerity as I was, I felt sympathetic to the horror that Lillian and her entire family were going through. There was a slight possibility that Jason would deliver on his promise to sell Ray's story and be able to bring them some small sense of peace.

I also knew that if I refused, Ray would just move on to another bail-bond agent and arrange the same thing. I knew what Jason was capable of and figured that if I was on the case, at least I could monitor Jason's actions. Babysit him, if you will. If he pulled a fast one, I wouldn't let him get away with it.

Against my better judgment, I let Lillian sign on her house to secure Jason's bail and he was released. It's not always necessary for me to meet with clients once they've been let out of custody, but I made a point to see Jason in person. I wanted to be able to look him in the eye.

"You're going to make all of your court appearances, right Jason?" I asked him.

"Absolutely, Chickie. Absolutely."

Well, it came as no surprise when Jason missed his first court appearance. *What a schmuck.*

I had assumed this was what would happen and had already made preliminary contact with a bounty hunter. Time was ticking and the house Lillian had put up for collateral was in serious danger of being forfeited. I was not about to let that happen.

I called the bounty hunter and told him to find Jason. There was no way he was going to con his way out of this one. The chase was on.

Flipping through my rolodex of business contacts, I found the name of someone I'd known in high school who had become a pretty big deal at a Hollywood movie studio. Growing up in Los Angeles had its perks.

I called my old friend, and we caught up for a few minutes. Then I got into it. "I'm looking for a man about 5'8, skinny, and blond. Goes by the name of Jason Westmorland."

It was a longshot. The chances of Jason weaseling his way into a big movie studio were slim. "Oh yeah—he was here the other day—great guy!" *Great guy?! Ha!* Jason certainly was Mr. Charm—I'll give him that. I had to give him a little credit. I didn't think he would try to go through with his scheme. Jason must have thought there was money in it for him—he certainly didn't do it out of the kindness of his heart.

Although a good con man, Jason turned out to be a terrible fugitive. It didn't take long for the bounty hunter to find him. Jason was hiding out in the apartment of one of his girlfriends—of which he had many. The bounty hunter brought Jason back into custody, right where he belonged.

Alas, the cop's story to clear his name would remain untold, but at the very least his wife got her house back—the only happy ending you could hope for in such a sordid circumstance.

I did eventually receive the premium for the bond. However, the bounty hunter charged me 10 percent of the bail amount, and I had no choice but to pay him. My premium went to him, and I was left with zero. I could have foreclosed on the property for this amount but there was no way I would do that.

My payment was knowing that Lillian and her children were able to keep their home. There was no way I would have taken anything from her. Everything had been taken from her already. How could I take anything more?

I thought I had seen the last of Jason Westmorland, but a bad penny always turns up. Years later I was attending a charity function for Beit Tu Shuva, an organization close to my heart that saves the lives of those fighting addictions. A strange man came running up to me and excitedly shook my hand, "Chickie, how wonderful to see you!"

I had no idea who he was.

"It's Jason Westmorland."

This man bore no resemblance to the lanky, blond kid I remembered. He had gained some weight, his hair was now black, and he had a beard—but the overly charming personality was the same. Same mischievous twinkle in his eye.

Jason apologized profusely for all the aggravation he had caused me, insisting he wanted to make amends. "I want to pay you back for that bail bond premium. What's your number, Chickie?"

I could feel my eyes wanting to roll back into my head, but I gave Jason the benefit of the doubt. Reluctantly, I gave him my number and he left, promising to call the next day to "make things right." I didn't plan to lose any sleep waiting for that call. I knew who I was dealing with. I contemplated that perhaps he had dyed his hair and grown a beard as some kind of disguise or maybe it was part of his new scam. With con artists like Jason, everything is calculated—especially their appearance.

As I watched Jason flutter around the room that night, chatting up all sorts of people, I couldn't help but wonder what kind of new scheme he was trying to pull, who would become his next victim. Of course, he never called.

-7-

THE BIKER AND THE BOX OF CHOCOLATES

I have to go bail out a motorcycle gang member," I announced to Fred at our Santa Monica condo one rainy evening before Christmas.

This would be Chickie's Bail Bonds first Christmas! I had been busy assembling holiday gifts for our criminal defense attorneys when the call came in from a strange lawyer, but business is business. I was happy to drive the half-hour to the Long Beach Jail in the rain to impress this new lawyer and to make the $50.00 premium on a $500.00 bond. Who knows what future referrals this might lead to?

I was starting to get used to the unpredictable lifestyle of a bail-bond agent. The late nights, the missing out on events, being at the beck and call of my business 24/7. However, the holidays were when I noticed it the most. I loved being with family, but crime never takes a day off—so neither did I. Just a few weeks earlier I had put our Thanksgiving turkey in the oven when the phone rang—and the rest is history. I may not have enjoyed my holiday dinner, but I certainly helped another family enjoy theirs!

"Big Mike" Parker was a member of the Vagos motorcycle gang with a rap sheet as long as a traffic jam on a Los Angeles freeway. He had recently been arrested for an FTA (failure to appear) in an ongoing case, charges which included trying to bribe an officer of the law.

The Vagos were as dangerous an outlaw motorcycle gang as gangs got. Sometimes referred to as "the mafia on wheels," they were right up there with the Hells Angels.

Despite the Vagos maintaining they were a legitimate motorcycle club, members were notorious for drug running, illegal weapons sales, robbery, and there were even allegations of murder. Of course they would never refer to themselves as "gangs," and they did have quite a few members with no criminal records. Some Vagos members were even known to hand out toys at Christmas.

No matter how dangerous a defendant might be, I knew I was protected. Technically, jail was one of the safest places I could be since it was teeming with police. It was not like I was going to be alone with the defendant or anything like that.

As I headed out, I glanced at our dining room table now cluttered with a festive mountain of ribbons, tape, and bows. I clocked how many mugs still needed to be put together. I was delighted with how attractive our newly designed "Chickie mugs" were! With their first morning cup of coffee, our attorneys would see a happy little chick bursting out of bent prison bars. A good way to start the day. We may not have been able to afford expensive gifts our first year in business, but they would certainly be unique—just as our business was! This was an important step in building my business relationships, and as my business grew, so did my gift-giving.

Our second year in business I created holiday baskets of Chickie mugs plus coffee beans, a coffee grinder, and assorted sweets. We were moving up in the world! It was a big job, so I got my son Mitch and Fred to help assemble them—plus Mitch and Fred had to drive all over LA delivering. After an exhausting day Fred told me in no uncertain terms, "Never again—find another way to say thank you!"

And so, we did.

Our third year in business we threw a Holiday Thank You Party in a reasonably priced restaurant. With every following year, our business increased and our parties became more and more elaborate. We were finally able to appropriately express our appreciation to the lawyers who supported us.

Admittedly, I was nervous about the idea of getting a group of potential adversaries together at an event. How would they react being in the same room as their competition? My concerns were groundless—there was great camaraderie among the lawyers, and they all expressed their thanks for bringing them together in such a great social setting.

Over the years, many of them would tell me they looked forward to "the first Thursday in November" where Chickie's Bail Bonds kicked off the holiday season. We continued this tradition for over three decades—and I have the photos to prove it!

Still thinking about my holiday plans, I got into my car to meet my new Vagos client. Luckily, at this time of night the Los Angeles freeways were wide open. Buildings were just beginning to show off their Christmas decorations. Carols were already being sung on every radio station. "It's the Most Wonderful Time of the Year" was playing, and there I was, contemplating my drive home from the jail.

The holiday season was the time of the year for families to be together, and my conundrum was that I had to sacrifice time with my family in order to help take care of them. Although Mitch and my daughter Karen understood, I think Fred was annoyed by it all. He didn't seem to fully grasp that I was doing it for him.

As a child, I felt being Jewish set me apart from the other kids. I was envious of the Christian kids who had Christmas. They enjoyed the beauty of decorated Christmas trees with gaily wrapped packages and the fragrant smell of pine permeating their homes—while I had none of it. When teachers would ask what I hoped Santa would bring me I would have to explain that my family didn't celebrate Christmas. It always made me feel left out.

I was raised being proud of my Jewish heritage and celebrating the important Jewish holidays: Passover and Rosh Hashanah. Lesser holidays, like Chanukah, were not observed in a household with limited funds for "extras" like gifts.

As an adult, I've gone in the opposite direction. I have chosen to pass my heritage on to my children by celebrating not only the important Jewish holidays but Chanukah as well with its beautiful traditions of eight nights of candle lighting and gift giving. My own family lights the Chanukah candles each night and reads our treasured Chanukah children's book as we have from the time Karen was born—its worn pages reflecting all the happy years of our enjoyment. Traditional potato latkes are always served with sour cream and applesauce. I would say it was just like mom used to make, but that's a claim best made by my kids. I'm proud of that.

I waited almost an hour as the Long Beach Jail clerks took more time than usual to process my defendant, perhaps short-staffed due to the upcoming holidays. One thing was for sure—I didn't want to have to stay there all night. Jail was unpleasant. They made it unpleasant. And it was always ice cold.

Impatiently, I tapped my French-manicured nails on my briefcase, watching the rotating cast of characters pass by, from prostitutes and drug dealers to people who looked as if they could be your neighbor.

When an intimidating hairy hulk of a man emerged through the jail door there was no question that it was him. He was the quintessential motorcycle gang member: beer-bellied with bushy hair, a long scraggly beard, and a thick pelt of dark chest hair. And no shirt—just a tight leather vest that had no chance of ever meeting in the middle. The back of his vest sported the triangle insignia of Loki, the Norse God of mischief, and the front was adorned with a variety of green patches that I later learned signified Vagos members' achievements—criminal and otherwise. I maintained my composure as I approached this gargantuan man. He was just another client who needed my help.

"Good evening, I'm Chickie from Chickie's Bail Bonds. I

posted your five-hundred-dollar bail bond at the request of your attorney."

Expecting him to be volatile or crude, Big Mike was surprisingly convivial and—dare I say—*sweet?* He thanked me profusely for getting him out.

It was almost two o'clock in the morning when I finished with his paperwork and I was eager to get home. To pay for my services, Big Mike pulled out a giant wad of cash and peeled off five ten-dollar bills. I thought it was unusual for someone to be walking around with that much money, but I happily pocketed my fifty dollars and headed back to my car.

Pulling out of the jail parking lot, it was still pouring rain, and I needed to find the nearest freeway back to Los Angeles. Out of the corner of my eye, I spotted Big Mike sitting on the jail steps all by himself absolutely drenched. *He must be cold,* I thought—especially without a shirt.

Slowly, I drove up to him and rolled down my window. "Do you need a ride somewhere?"

"Yeah, if you don't mind. I'm not far away."

He got into my car, placing his dripping motorcycle helmet down next to him. It was a dark gun-metal gray, reminiscent of the ones military storm troopers would wear. We sat in silence for a moment as I contemplated how I could possibly had invited a Vagos motorcycle gang member into my car in the middle of the night … like an idiot.

What was I supposed to do? Leave this man stranded there and have to ask one of the Vagos members to come all the way out there at this time of night? I felt this was part of my job. After all, I did just make fifty dollars. That was a big deal in those days!

"Seatbelt." I gently instructed him.

"Yes, ma'am," he said as he fumbled around. Wearing a seatbelt wasn't the law at the time—but if you were in my car, it was.

Despite our stark contrast in physical appearance, to say

nothing of our chosen professions, in a way he seemed more intimidated by me than I was of him. He was incredibly appreciative and respectful. Always "yes ma'am" or "no ma'am." With bail an all-male industry, he wasn't expecting anyone like me to show up! As a mother I have found that most people have an inherent respect for maternal figures. Everyone has a mother.

Driving away from Long Beach jail, Big Mike proceeded to give me directions to the house where he lived. In retrospect, he could have been leading me to Vagos' headquarters or somewhere equally perilous.

I had no idea what would come out of my mouth except I knew I needed to keep talking to keep my mind off the thought of any imminent danger.

"hope Santa will get you for Christmas?"

I could feel Big Mike turn in his seat to stare at me, somewhat taken aback by my innocent question. He let out a hearty laugh.

"I don't know. I haven't really been a good boy this year."

"I hope Santa brings me See's Candies," I continued. "The holidays are the one time of year when I indulge without guilt."

I asked Big Mike if he was going to do anything special for Christmas. He said he wasn't really religious but that he was looking forward to celebrating. I mentioned that my family wasn't particularly religious especially my husband who always said, "Maybe God wanted me to be an atheist." Big Mike seemed to get a kick out of that.

Big Mike asked me to drop him in front of a decrepit apartment complex—several poorly constructed buildings slumped against each other like tired soldiers trying to remain erect. As he exited my car Mike expressed his sincere thanks for the ride as he dashed out through the pouring rain.

"Don't forget to show up for your court appearance," I hollered as he got out of my car. Big Mike's wave assured me that he absolutely would and I believed him.

A couple of months later I received a forfeiture notice in the mail indicating that Big Mike did not show up and I was livid. Not only had he broken his promise to the court, he had broken his promise to me. I was furious! If I wasn't able to track him down it was going to cost me five hundred dollars. I knew where he lived, but I wasn't about to just show up at such a precarious location. Who knows what I would possibly encounter?

The smartest move was to call his attorney and get to the bottom of it. I dialed his number, determined to get some answers. But after several days and numerous unreturned phone calls, I realized I was getting the runaround from this two-bit lawyer.

When I called the court to obtain more details about Big Mike's case status, I was informed that Mike had appeared late causing the bond to be forfeited; he had not skipped out.

Regardless, the forfeiture was still on the books. In those days the only way to erase the forfeiture and its resultant penalty was to have an attorney go into court on my behalf and file a motion to set aside the forfeiture. It would be as if it never happened. Like magic.

Fortunately, I knew Ed Fitzgerald—an attorney who specialized in rescuing bail agents from this exact type of situation. For fifty dollars he was happy to head into court and file the appropriate motion that would save me from having to pay the full amount of the bond: $500.00.

Fifty dollars was my full premium which meant after I paid the attorney I would have worked for nothing.

I had to figure out how to track down Big Mike and get him to reimburse me the money I had to pay for his mistake. What's right is right and when it came to money, I always went after what I was owed.

Early on when Fred and I were first married, I was a stay-at-home mom and was facing the very real challenge of how to make ends meet. I took a cold-calling job from home, selling what I said were quality mattresses at discount prices. It was a doozy! The daily hostility I encountered from each furious person who in many cases left the comfort of their couch and television set to answer the ringing phone in the other room!

This was way before cell phones existed and homes had only one phone. If I was lucky, I'd just hear the slam of the phone receiver, otherwise I'd get an earful of profanity.

Every once in a while, my persistence managed to convince some kind soul to agree to have one of our salesmen do an in-home presentation, no obligation, of course, which meant that yours truly would receive a commission of ten whole dollars. Boy, was I elated!

There was one time when the company denied me the ten-dollar commission I had earned for a successful cold call. I took it up with management but to no avail—likely because I was a very young woman and they thought they could take advantage of the situation, that I would simply back down. They were wrong. I took them to court on my own and won my ten dollars! I had worked hard for that money and wasn't going to be cheated out of it. Nor would I be cheated out of the fifty dollars that Big Mike had cost me.

I knew Big Mike hadn't skipped town, so I didn't need a bounty hunter. I deduced that if the Vagos motorcycle gang was as legitimate as they claimed, it should be listed in the phone book. Would you believe that one of America's most notorious outlaw motorcycle gangs was listed in the *Yellow Pages*? It was right there, under Motorcycle Clubs.

Not sure where this would go, I picked up the phone, dialed their number, and asked to speak to the president. The man who answered the call was dismissive and I could hear him mutter to someone in the background, "It's some lady ... I don't know ... she says she's owed some money?"

A man with a gravelly voice picked up the phone. "Who is this?"

I was speaking to the president of the Vagos motorcycle gang.

I was no pushover; I told him exactly how one of his members had messed up and that I was now out fifty dollars. He became outraged at Big Mike and said in no uncertain terms that his organization did not tolerate such unacceptable behavior from its members. He promised that I would be hearing from his wayward club member right away.

True to his word, the very next day I received a contrite phone call from Big Mike who apologized profusely and offered to meet me right away to settle up what he owed.

We met for coffee at Mel's Diner on Ventura Boulevard—an iconic 50s style diner that still stands there today.

We sat across from each other in a booth and I'm sure we were quite a sight: a petite middle-aged Jewish woman and a biker-gang behemoth. Big Mike apologized once again and gave me the money he owed. He also presented me with a belated Christmas gift: a giant box of See's Candies. I was astonished. He remembered what I had told him during our car ride.

As we said our goodbyes and exchanged holiday wishes, Big Mike told me, "If you ever have trouble collecting money from anyone, just call me."

My face must have looked shocked because he immediately explained that he doesn't actually hurt anyone. "It's just that when they see me, somehow they come up with the money."

We both had a chuckle. I almost believed him.

I never heard from Big Mike after that, but within a year I did receive a call from his lawyer who had disappeared when I needed him. I'm a firm believer that what goes around comes around and now the shoe was on the other foot. Mr. Fancy Shmancy Lawyer who wouldn't return my calls was in custody and begged for my help to get him released.

I simply hung up the phone with a big smile on my face.

A GOODY TWO-SHOES WALKS INTO A DRUG DEN

I always felt that it was necessary to come across as professional as possible—even at a drug den. No matter where I was going or what time it was, I always made sure to put on my black pantsuit, grab my briefcase, and look like a businesswoman—nevermind that in this case I was going to be dealing with scumbags.

This event took place on a chilly February night—although it might be more accurate to say morning. It was about 2 a.m. and I was in Orange County standing on a quiet street, bleary-eyed and exhausted. Suffice to say I was not my usual perky self.

A drug den is a house or apartment used in the illegal drug trade frequented by those buying and/or consuming illegal drugs. These are often abandoned properties prized by drug dealers, usually secluded with no rent receipts to form a paper trail. They were run by men, guarded by men, and frequented mostly by men … and they often had guns.

I, on the other hand, have never carried a gun or mace or anything. Regardless of the circumstance, I never feel in danger. I'm trying to help someone so why would anyone want to hurt me? Even walking to my car late at night I've never felt afraid. That's just who I am. I also found many of my clients very protective, walking me to my car and cautioning me to lock my doors.

I was going to this drug den to collect a significant amount of cash to post bail for two defendants who had been arrested on drug charges. Lester Harris, also known as Spoony, was covering the bail for his "associates." Following a short discussion of the particulars, the defendant's attorney Gilbert Geilum gave me the address.

If my son Mitch had known what I was doing, he would have had a fit. He was very protective of his mother and didn't like me running around late at night. He certainly would have tried to talk me out of going to an unsavory part of town to meet with drug dealers. Fred, on the other hand, was usually sound asleep when I ventured out. I never bothered to tell him where I was going. I would just steal away in the middle of the night, hopefully back in time to make him his breakfast and coffee in the morning. He didn't need to know.

Glancing down at my trusty yellow notepad, I double-checked the address. This was it. From the outside, it looked like a regular house, but as I got closer, I could see the exterior paint was peeling off and several of the windows were boarded up.

I had no idea what awaited me on the other side of the door. I just stood there in mute anticipation thinking to myself, *Chickie, you can do this. This is a great opportunity. You're going to make some money and impress this new lawyer.*

Allan Kinsman was a criminal defense attorney whom I had met at Terminal Island Correctional Facility just a couple of weeks before. There was a large waiting room with roughly fifty chairs around. The only seat taken was filled by a well-dressed gentleman, no doubt an attorney waiting for his client.

From the inception of Chickie's Bail Bonds, I was constantly looking to add to my roster of attorneys. Although there were 49 other chairs to choose from, I decided to seize the opportunity and plunked myself down next to him.

I was right! He was an attorney waiting to see his client. Alan said he had a small firm specializing in criminal defense, located in Santa Monica, not far from where my home office was.

Allan told me that he and Attorney Gilbert Geilum often required the services of a bail agent and that they didn't have an attachment to one in particular. I smiled to myself and thought, *Well, you're about to have one now!*

I didn't even wait 24 hours before calling the office to set up a meeting. There was no need to be coy. Alan had seemed genuinely interested as we were talking and I wanted to strike while the iron was hot.

After several unanswered messages I decided to just show up at the office. The staff seemed somewhat disorganized; however, I noticed one employee actually working. It was apparent to me that, whereas Alan Kinsman had the office and reputation, Gilbert Geilum was the real power behind the throne.

Gilbert's office door was open, so I went in and introduced myself. I gave him my pitch and he was very receptive. Gilbert told me that he handled most of the cases and was the one who called bail agents when their clients needed to be released from custody. He echoed Alan's statement that they didn't have one specific bail bond agent that they worked with.

Gilbert must have been impressed by my tenacity because he called me within a week requesting my services for one of his clients. It was going to be a real test of my abilities.

"Are you familiar with drug dens?" Gilbert asked over the phone.

"Of course."

Familiar, yes. But had I ever been to one before? Absolutely not.

Any other woman probably would have hung up the phone as soon as they heard the words "drug den" but that thought would never occur to me. I've always felt that you can be a success in your life if you're willing to work hard and take advantage of every opportunity even if it seems outrageous or even beneath you.

I knocked on the door of the unassuming house. In the dead of night, I could hear the murmurs of people shuffling around inside. I didn't have to wait long before the door slowly creaked open, revealing a disheveled man in his mid-40s with heavily pock-marked skin and a long, greasy ponytail.

"Hello, I'm Chickie from Chickie's Bail Bonds. Are you Spoony?"

He nodded while he sized me up with a decided smirk, "*You're the bail agent?*"

Spoony's heavy-lidded eyes were swollen and red. Clearly, he had been sampling the merchandise.

"Come in."

As soon as I entered the house, I was engulfed in a haze of cigarette and marijuana smoke. The living room was dimly lit with candles and littered with drug paraphernalia: a few needles, scattered pieces of tinfoil, and half-empty cans of food and pizza boxes were piled in disarray on the coffee table.

A few people were scattered around the room on a dilapidated sofa and easy chair; some were lying down. I couldn't tell if they were sleeping or strung out on drugs. If any of them were actually drug dealers, their shabby appearances indicated they weren't very successful ones.

Spoony escorted me to what was supposed to be the kitchen. "For privacy," he said.

With one sweep of his arm, all that littered the kitchen table landed on the floor, making space for the paperwork I needed him to sign. I gingerly sat on one of the kitchen chairs, mentally making a note to strip all of my clothes as soon as I got home, bag them, and send them to the cleaners.

Once the papers were signed, guaranteeing the appearance of the two defendants in court, Spoony stood up, rocking back and forth on his heels as he conferred with an extremely skinny man wearing multiple chains around his neck.

"Wait here," Spoony said abruptly as he slinked upstairs, leaving me standing to face the room full of men in various drug-induced states. They were all grinning ear-to-ear at my visible discomfort. They could see I clearly did not belong there.

"Wanna sit down?" said a man with a bright red mohawk as he patted an empty space beside him on the sofa. It was covered in trash and cigarette butts.

"No, thank you."

In junior high I was known as a goody two-shoes. I didn't drink or smoke and I dressed modestly—unlike most of my girlfriends. In the 40s it was very trendy to smoke cigarettes. All the movie stars smoked. The cool kids in school all smoked. It was rebellious, even sexy.

My girlfriends would come over to my house after school and smoke cigarettes because my mother didn't care. My friends all thought my mother was cool because their parents would have been outraged at their kids smoking.

My mother smoked constantly so she didn't think it made sense to tell others that they couldn't. She always smoked Chesterfields. I remember she would sit at the kitchen table at the window, coffee in one hand, a flickering cigarette in the other. Often, she would be doing her makeup in the morning as she got ready for work; the Chesterfield cigarette always there. That was very important to her. I, on the other hand, never had the desire to even try a cigarette. And I never have.

"Come on, you at least want a smoke?" The man with the mohawk grabbed the freshest looking extinguished cigarette from his ash tray and waved it in my general direction.

"No, thank you."

Spoony reappeared with a large brown paper bag, overflowing

with crumpled-up cash. I had been told in advance that this would be a cash transaction, but I didn't really think about what $220,000 would look like. The bail to be posted was for two $100,000 bonds. Since the collateral guaranteeing the bonds was in cash, I needed to hold $200,000 as collateral, plus my premium of $20,000.

Spoony thrust the bag of money toward me. "How much is in there?" I asked.

"I don't know," Spoony snickered as he exchanged glances with the men on the couch. They were all very amused. "You'll have to count it."

Count it?! My stomach dropped. I had never been able to count money on a good day, and here it was coming up on three in the morning, in a smoke-laden drug house, surrounded by thugs. But it was imperative that I remain confident and show Alan Kinsman and Gilbert Geilum that they had made the right decision working with me.

"Fine. Where can I count it?"

Spoony led me down a dark hallway into a bedroom that smelled like mildew and was sparsely furnished with a decrepit set of drawers and a "bed" that was nothing more than a box spring with a stained mattress haphazardly thrown on top.

This wasn't the ideal place to count money, but I didn't have much of a choice.

"Watch the door," Spoony growled to a bulky-looking man whom I surmised was a guard.

This man was covered in tattoos and wore a muscle shirt with exposed forearms that hinted of prior needle usage. He wasn't there to protect me—he was there to protect the money.

Spoony left the room and I heard the door lock with a loud click. It was just me, the guard, and the money.

I poured the huge paper bag out onto the bed, watching waves of twenties, fifties, and hundreds spill out over the mattress, like a sea of green. There were even some fives, tens, and single dollar bills in the mix.

This was going to take a while.

I had no confidence in myself at that moment, but I had to put on an air of bravado. I took a deep breath and started counting. *One hundred ... two hundred ... two hundred and twenty ... two hundred and twenty-five ...*

At the rate I was going this was going to take all night! It was infuriating! I just plodded along hoping for the best. *Three hundred and twenty-five ... three hundred and seventy-five ...*

Despite the fact that I was surrounded by drug dealers, junkies, and foul-smelling carpets soaked with blood stains and urine, I wasn't really affected by any of it. I was there to do a job.

When I was sixteen and able to get a work permit, I obtained secretarial part-time employment at the Pelphrey Rabbit Company—a corporation in Los Angeles that processed rabbits for transport to markets for human consumption. Apparently, there was a big market for rabbits at the time.

I was still in high school but loved the independence of going to work. I took the streetcar every day after school to the office where I practiced my newfound abilities—taking shorthand and typing. It made me feel like a grown up and I enjoyed having the new responsibility.

On the first day of work, Mr. Pelphrey gave me a tour of the office and walked me into the refrigerated room where the employees were preparing the dead rabbits. Nothing could have prepared me for the overwhelmingly vile stench! Instinctively, my hands flew up to cover my mouth and nose. Oh, it was horrendous!

I watched the workers handling the rabbits—positioning their floppy bodies into cardboard boxes—it all seemed so shockingly routine for them. Rabbits were freshly killed and brought to the factory each day for processing and sale. I remember I couldn't imagine those cute little bunnies being skewered on a barbecue when they could have been dear pets to people, but who was I to judge?

The odor of the refrigerated room was so dreadful I couldn't wait to get back to the office. Suppressing my need to vomit had to be one of my most successful achievements at that job. Every few days my duties would require me to venture into the refrigerated room again, but I never complained. I was there to do a job. I would find a way to put up with the smell.

One year later, in my senior year at Roosevelt High School, my involvement in school and extracurricular social activities made me reluctantly decide to leave the Pelphrey Rabbit Company.

On my last day I stepped into the refrigerated room to say goodbye to my work friends and a peculiar thing occurred. I noticed that the revolting odor I had encountered on my first day was completely gone. I didn't have to cover my nose and mouth because I no longer smelled the dead rabbits. In fact, I smelled nothing.

The dead rabbit smell was indeed still there; however, I ascertained that the repeated exposure from working on the premises had somehow made me immune to it.

That which becomes familiar has the power to change one's perception.

When I finally finished counting Spoony's bag of money I was surprised to discover that there was a surplus of $3,000. I thought that I had counted correctly and I certainly wasn't about to start over. I neatly packed the collateral and premium money back into the paper bag, keeping the excess cash separate.

The tattooed guard escorted me back to the living room where some new "customers" had arrived and were milling about. With the bag tucked securely under my arm, I gave Spoony a Chickie's Bail

Bonds receipt for the money I had received and handed him the extra money, informing him there was an extra $3,000 in the bag. He happily accepted the cash, but I couldn't help noticing that he had an odd look on his face.

Pleased to be away from the drug den, I got in my car to drive home to secure the cash before I headed to the jail to post the two bonds for the release of Gilbert's clients—Spoony's associates. I had earned $20,000, which was incredible to me, and most assuredly I had impressed the new lawyers. Yet I couldn't stop thinking about the $3,000 overage.

It wasn't until I was halfway home that it dawned on me.

Chickie, you fool. There was no way that there would have been more money in that bag than what was due to me. Those guys may have been drug dealers, but they were not stupid and would never have given me more money than what they had to.

There were no two ways about it. I must have miscounted.

I continued to berate myself the entire way home, becoming more and more incensed. I was mad at myself for only counting the money once and I was furious with Spoony for taking the $3,000.

It was a little after 5 a.m. when I arrived home and stormed into the house. "Fred!" I yelled. He was still sleeping, but I was so mad that I didn't give it a thought. I flipped on the bedroom lights. "Fred, wake up!"

Disoriented, Fred fumbled for his glasses perched on the bedside table. "What time is it?" he groaned.

"Five in the morning," I said tersely and dumped the bag of money onto the bed.

"Count it!"

Fred knew from my tone not to ask any more questions and he got to work. As an engineer he was very methodical and good with numbers, making him a far better money counter than me. There was so much pent-up frustration racing through my veins that I began to pace the room. Fred's method was far more systematic than what I had done. When the last of the bills had been counted, he alerted me that it was $3,000 short—the exact amount I had returned to Spoony.

I knew it!

Giving Fred a quick thank you, I let him go back to sleep and ran to the kitchen to get Spoony on the phone. I was so angry I could burst! Not surprisingly he was still awake. I proceeded to give him what for. After I was through with my tirade there was a brief silence followed by the sound of hysterical laughter. Spoony thought the entire thing was so funny! When it comes to being short changed, I saw no humor in it at all.

I wasn't about to head back to Orange County to collect the difference. I'm not sure I could collect it if I did. But the joke was on him! I had his $200,000 cash and when it came time to return his collateral, it was just a matter of reducing it by $3,000.

When a case is over and the bond exonerated by the court, the bail bond is no longer needed, and the collateral the bail agent is holding, in this case $200,000, is returned to the depositor.

The next time I met Spooney was in court, where he obviously realized the need to appear normal, not the dreadful mess of a strung-out druggy. He had even done something with his awful hair—it was no longer all over the place.

Just as Spoony reached for the $200,000 cash collateral, I reminded him that he owed me $3,000. I immediately removed it from the $200,000. Spoony suddenly had this funny look on his face as though he had forgotten. But I sure didn't, and happily walked away with the $3,000 clenched tightly in my fist and a smile on my face.

This excruciating incident taught me two valuable lessons in the bail-bond industry. First, I learned that I needed to know how to count money the right way. I went to my bank and learned directly from one of the tellers. And second, I learned that I didn't actually need to count the money. No one ever hands over significant amounts of cash unless they know the exact amount—to the penny.

From that day forward whenever I am taking cash from a client, I rarely bother to count it. When a client says to me, "Aren't you going to count the money?" I always respond with, "Well, didn't you count it?"

The answer is always, "Of course I counted it." So, I reply with, "Well then, why do I have to?"

In all my years in business, the amount has always been exactly correct.

-9-

MITCH AND THE SEX PRIESTESS

I was as surprised as anyone that my son Mitch hilariously ended up in a newspaper photo with the self-proclaimed sex priestess of the Church of the Most High Goddess. The caption read: "Mary Ellen Tracy and husband walking out of the courtroom."

Although pictured together on the steps of the Los Angeles County Courthouse, Mitch was there representing Chickie's Bail Bonds. He was most certainly not this woman's husband.

By the end of the 1980s, Chickie's Bail Bonds had become firmly established, the phone ringing off the hook with new business. My business strategy was paying off. I had created an expansive network of attorneys that were constantly sending both state and federal bonds our way. The volume was becoming too great for just one person to handle.

I knew that I needed someone who could represent Chickie's Bail Bonds appropriately, with a high standard of professionalism and ethics. Someone I could trust who had empathy for our clients and the utmost respect for the attorneys. In short, I needed an extension of me. Hiring my son, Mitch, just made perfect sense.

Mitch was in his early 20s and was a student at Santa Monica Junior College pursuing a career in broadcasting. He had aspirations to be involved in music and had a great speaking and singing voice. However, he was concerned about my going out alone on nighttime calls and had often accompanied me.

When I asked him to join the company full time, he very

willingly accepted the offer. Mitch officially became the first employee of Chickie's Bail Bonds. More than eager to help the family business, he immersed himself in studying all the materials necessary to become a licensed bail-bond agent and quickly earned his license. From there he hit the ground running.

From the get-go, Mitch insisted on handling the night calls by himself. I always felt he was making too big of a deal about it, but I appreciated being able to stay home at night, and I know Fred appreciated it as well.

Mitch was a natural at being a bail-bond agent. He loved dealing with people and had a knack for knowing the ins and outs of getting around Southern California.

Since Chickie's was known by its watchword: "Call Chickie—she comes to you," I needed someone who knew Los Angeles like the back of their hand. Even without a map and before GPS, Mitch could find his way anywhere in Los Angeles, Orange, and San Diego counties. Mitch hilariously found himself being called "Chickie" when meeting a client for the first time, thanks to our watchword.

I had always managed to get around but not like Mitch. One wrong exit off the freeway in Los Angeles and you've lost half an hour, which could mean the defendant spending more time in jail than necessary or our possibly losing the bond to another bail agent. It was my goal to make sure the defendant did not spend even one minute more than necessary in custody, one more way we endeared ourselves to the defendant's families and the referring attorney.

In the office I would hear Mitch speak to clients on the telephone using my exact words, making me feel I was hearing myself talk! I was so tickled! I learned that I could depend on him to handle many of the cases himself, leaving only the big stuff for me.

Mitch is one of the sweetest, kindest people I have ever known. When Mitch was growing up, I was working and didn't have as much time for him as I should have. He was the little boy that held onto his mommy and wouldn't let go, who went to nursery school, held onto the teacher, and wouldn't let go.

Fred would tell me to stop babying Mitch because he was a boy and needed to toughen up, not be so soft. Whereas I have always felt that you could get far more advantages in life by being soft than by being tough. Fred was the first male in my life. I was raised without a father or a brother, so when Fred insisted he knew best how to raise our son, I deferred to him.

At Chickie's Bail Bonds, Mitch's "softness"—his affability, warmth, and willingness to go the extra mile to help—was his strength. Attorneys and clients took to him and a few of the lawyers preferred to deal with Mitch over me, appreciating his eagerness to please. Mitch matured greatly from his daily dealings as a bail-bond agent, becoming well-known at the jails, well-liked, and respected.

With Mitch on board, Chickie's Bail Bonds continued to grow. Business was booming. We even had to hire a secretary to run the office and manage the clerical and administrative details. Both Mitch and I detested paperwork, so this was a welcome addition. We had staked our claim in the bail-bond industry, and no one could deny that a female-run agency was any less capable than one run by a male.

Fred was no longer telling me to "get a real job." In fact, it was me who convinced him to retire from *his* job at the Los Angeles County Road Department. I didn't see any sense in him wasting his energy going to work when I was generating enough income to support us. I thought it prudent that he spend whatever active time he had left doing what he loved—playing golf.

When Chickie's Bail Bonds outgrew our dining room table, we were able to afford Fred's dream home—a two-story condo on a golf course within walking distance of the beach. He couldn't believe it. I could hardly believe it myself. Quite a step up for a poor kid raised in Boyle Heights!

When we moved into our beautiful new home, Fred handed me a shiny red paper heart, a homemade card in his handwriting:

Chick, you made it happen. Love, Fred.

Up until that moment I had felt that Fred didn't fully believe in me. He had a hard time believing in anyone, even himself. Fred had given up college before he earned his degree when he was promised an exciting career designing Los Angeles highways. When the county ran out of money, he was relegated to designing fill for potholes—not his dream job and so far beneath him. But he never complained, not ever.

Of course, Fred rarely expressed his feelings about anything. It was his personality—he never complained about what a raw deal he had in his work and never expressed his feelings about Mitch and my success. Possibly, at the beginning, he couldn't believe what was happening. And when I insisted he retire, maybe he felt "less than," not realizing how happy I was in my work and that I was sincere that he didn't need to drag himself to a job he hated, especially as his condition worsened.

The condo was chosen specifically because there was an upstairs to be used as our offices. Chickie's Bail Bonds had always operated from my home, and we weren't about to change something that worked so well. The office could be a beehive of activity but was far enough away from our living area downstairs.

Working together with Mitch at Chickie's Bail Bonds brought us very close. In a way I felt we were making up for lost time. We would go to court together, work together on cases, and chat throughout the day about the goings on with clients.

One thing you learn in the bail bond industry is that it's unpredictable. You never knew what kind of person you were about to bail out of jail. On this particular day it happened to be the two leaders of a sex church. Yes, that's right—a sex church!

Mitch received the call from one of our attorneys representing the married couple Mary Ellen and Wilbur Tracy of The Church of the Most High Goddess. The attorney explained that this couple had been arrested and were being held in the Santa Monica Jail with bail set at $20,000 each.

A couple getting arrested for running a church could be for many reasons. Generally, the first thing you think of is some kind of financial malfeasance—that they're stealing from people or not filing the proper tax returns. It wasn't until this case was fully explained to me that I realized how ridiculous it really was.

Mary Ellen was being charged with prostitution while her husband Wilbur was accused of pimping. Well aware of the case's inherent absurdity, the attorney was more or less tongue-in-cheek, describing the events precipitating the arrest of the sex priestess.

This middle-aged married couple had been operating a special kind of "church" based upon the worship of Isis, the ancient Egyptian goddess of fertility. To be accepted into the church, believers donated large sums of money and were required to engage in sexual acts with the High Priestess, Mary Ellen Tracy.

This was certainly not something that I had ever heard of!

Mitch hung up the phone, and we both had a chuckle. Unfazed by the bizarre details of the case, Mitch was out the door within a few minutes, his car hurtling toward the Santa Monica jail.

When Mary Ellen Tracy appeared in court she was quite attractively dressed in what she claimed was the traditional attire for a high priestess of the Church of the Most High Goddess—a bright red sequined strapless dress, fishnet stockings, and black high heels. This was hardly what one would expect a defendant to wear for a court appearance, nor certainly not what one would consider professional, although she was being charged for prostitution, which *is* known as the world's oldest profession.

I couldn't help noticing the difficulty many of the male attorneys had in keeping a straight face as the defendant proclaimed her innocence due to her religious beliefs.

A defense attorney's job is to defend his client even when he sees the absurdity of her defense. I watched Mary Ellen's defense attorney as he tried to keep a straight face when his client in her sexy attire insisted on proclaiming her innocence.

Mary Ellen, who was referred to as Sabrina Aset by her followers, claimed she was not involved in prostitution but following her religious duty taking part in an ancient, misunderstood Egyptian religion where sexual rituals put men on the "path back to the divine."

The couple created the Church of the Most High Goddess after what they said was a divine revelation. They claimed there was a brilliant light through which knowledge was being poured into them without voice.

Because of the divine encounter, they began their church with precepts based on research into ancient Egyptian practices. Mary Ellen was a classical scholar with extensive knowledge in the area, and she took on the role of high priestess, whose divine duties included engaging in sexual intercourse with the church members. She claimed that the sex was done as part of a ritual of spiritual cleansing.

Wilbur was a high priest along with 10 others. Flourishing with over 2,000 male congregants, this church didn't have stained glass, pews, a pulpit, or even Bibles. It was just a four-bedroom rental home located near Beverly Hills, sparsely furnished with a few movie posters and a framed nude photograph of the high priestess herself, Mary Ellen Tracy.

A local newspaper had run a series of articles on this "new church," inadvertently attracting the attention of law enforcement. The articles included the fact that money was being offered in exchange for sexual favors, raising more than a few eyebrows. The Tracys were subsequently arrested.

When asked to provide a defense for her actions, Mary Ellen explained: "I have been deemed Sabrina Aset by the ancient gods and ordered by them to carry on the tradition of the Church of the Most High Goddess. I have been commanded to collect donations and to follow the ancient tradition of having sexual relations with my parishioners."

She went on to explain that prior to becoming a high priestess she had never had sex outside of marriage. "I've always been very willing to do what God required, whether to be monogamous or to have sex with a few thousand men," she said. "It really doesn't matter. I try to be accepting and open-minded."

Ridiculous as it was, it didn't shock or bother me in the least. I had come to accept the frailties of humans and to accept what's right for one person as opposed to what's right for the rest of the world. For the Tracys, this was the right thing to do. Until they got caught, of course.

***

When I was a teenager, my good friend, Shirley Resnick, fixed me up with her brother Sonny, four years my senior. The fact that he even asked me out was a minor miracle. We went on three dates: one, which involved my first ride on a motorcycle; two, when he took me to Monogram Studios for a screening of the film *The Red Shoes*; and three, when we went for a boat ride in Hollenbeck Park.

I was wearing one of my usual short-sleeved sweaters with a modest round neck. Every year I would go shopping with my girlfriends for our fall wardrobes and I would return home with basically the same outfit. "No, Chickie, low cut ... low cut," my mother would say in dismay as she went through my shopping bag. She probably thought a lowcut blouse would help me attract a boyfriend, but I didn't see myself that way at all. Being somewhat of a chubby girl I never liked to flaunt my body and much preferred to dress conservatively.

The boat ride was somewhat romantic. The sun was shining and water rippled below us. The trees in the distance gently swayed amidst a picturesque, blue cloudless sky. I was quite enjoying myself until Sonny dared to place his hand on my sweater-covered breast. I immediately slapped him across the face, abruptly ending our ill-fated romance.

The following week I convinced my mother to allow me to spend the weekend at my friend Niecie's house in West Los Angeles. Niecie, whose real name was Bernice Cohen, has been my dear friend since kindergarten and remains so.

While waiting for a streetcar on my way back home to Boyle Heights I observed two young men, also waiting for the streetcar, one of whom I recognized as an ex-boyfriend of one of my girlfriends. Jerry Levinson was a friend of the tall young man with him, Fred Leventhal. The three of us boarded the streetcar and I decided I wanted to get to know Fred better.

Knowing my mother had a package of calf's liver in the refrigerator, I invited Fred and Jerry to my family's apartment for a dinner of liver and onions. We had a wonderful dinner and a pleasant evening, listening to music, laughing, and dancing.

The following week I was thrilled when Fred asked me out. I remember thinking it was rather strange that he invited me to the Ambassador Hotel for our first date. It was a lovely hotel where non-guests could enjoy the use of the pool by paying a small fee. Fred explained he liked the poolside atmosphere, although later confessed he had chosen the location because he wanted to see what I looked like in a bathing suit.

Later we went to a local barbecue restaurant. Fred was the perfect gentleman, although at one point he brought up the subject of sex. Flustered, I tried to appear more sophisticated than I really was, acting as if I knew what he was talking about.

Oh sure, I managed to gasp out, everyone knows all about that—and quickly grabbed a glass of water to guzzle down hoping there was not going to be a tutorial on the subject I knew nothing about.

Throughout their trial, the Tracys contended that their activities were protected by the First Amendment. However, after three and a half days of deliberations, a Superior Court jury found Mary Ellen Tracy guilty of prostitution, rejecting the argument that she was being persecuted because of her religious beliefs. The jury felt that the prosecution had proved beyond a reasonable doubt that the defendants had broken the law.

"I am not a prostitute," Mary Ellen said defiantly after the verdict. "I'm very hurt by that. I'm a very sincere and honest person. To be portrayed as some kind of money-grubbing schemer is really devastating." When asked whether she would continue practicing her religion she said, "I am a high priestess and I have been ordained for life."

Mary Ellen was fined $3,000 and her husband Wilbur fined $1,000. They each served brief prison terms. Years later, Mary Ellen Tracy was involved in pornographic films. She also became something of a personality on the TV talk show circuit in the 1990s, appearing on *Donahue* and *The Montel Williams Show*—always outfitted in the same outlandish bright red sequined dress, fishnet stockings, and black high heels.

The following day the Tracys' verdict was all over the papers. One article in particular showed a photo of the high priestess, Mary Ellen, leaving the courthouse decked out in her red sequined dress and fishnet stockings. I was taken aback when I saw that behind her in the photo was Mitch, mistakenly labeled as her husband. I immediately telephoned Mitch to tell him about it, and we had a good laugh.

That night Fred, Mitch, and I went out to dinner at the local Italian restaurant Fred liked. Between devouring bites of pasta, Mitch and I caught up on our current cases, as we often did, including Mitch's recent brush with fame.

"What's a nice Jewish boy like you doing with a sex priestess?" I joked, referencing the photo. Mitch instantly burst into one of his high-pitched infectious laughs. As Mitch and I continued to prattle on about the case I heard Fred grumble from across the table, "What am I, chopped liver?"

Realizing that Fred felt left out, Mitch and I turned our attention to him, hearing all about Fred's day on the golf course. It was unfortunate that he was never able to take interest in Chickie's Bail Bonds—really sad for him.

I've always thought that the best definition of happiness is "wanting what you have." And that's what I had achieved. I was enjoying life, grateful for everything that I had. Chickie's Bail Bonds, which I had started to help support my family, had given me a chance at a rewarding career. But it had also given me a second chance at a better relationship with my son and an opportunity to do something meaningful for society. The Sixth Amendment declares an arrestee innocent until being brought before the court and declared guilty—and an innocent person should not have to remain in custody. That's where I came in with a smile on my face.

-10-

THE LONG
GOODBYE

As soon as I saw that Fred's car wasn't in the garage, I knew something was wrong.

I had been at a UCLA art exhibition that afternoon—not the sort of thing Fred was interested in—and was expecting to have a quiet night in with my husband.

Entering the front door I was surprised to be met with total darkness. "Fred," I called out, placing my keys on the table, "are you home?" I heard my voice echo down the hall. But no answer came. Since retiring, Fred spent his days on the golf course and at the gym, but he was always back in time for dinner. Always.

I checked the bedroom. Pitch black except for the tiny red light from my answering machine, beckoning me to a new message. *Blink! Blink! Blink!*

The red light continued to flash. I pressed the button and within seconds my entire world shattered.

"We are looking for the family of Fred Leventhal. This is the emergency room at UCLA Harbor Hospital…"

It felt as if time had stopped. *Oh no. This can't be.*

My heart was pounding as I managed to dial the number to the hospital. I spoke into the phone receiver in an anguished voice I barely recognized as my own. I was told that Fred had been hit by a drunk driver and was in critical condition. The doctor's voice on the phone was calm but firm. "You need to get to the hospital as soon

103

as possible."

Any uncertainty I had about the seriousness of the situation was removed. It was bad.

Frantic, I telephoned Mitch and told him that his father was in the hospital. We both knew I could not possibly drive. Mitch immediately came to pick me up.

The twenty-minute drive to the hospital felt like an eternity. Every red light, every stop sign was torture. I tried to remain optimistic, but I couldn't shake the feeling that what was said over the phone wasn't nearly as bad as what we were about to learn.

Everything after we arrived at the hospital was a blur until the emergency room doctor approached us. I clutched Mitch's hand tightly as the doctor explained that a drunk driver had crashed into Fred's red Toyota. A team of firemen had to use the jaws of life to pry open the roof of the mangled car and free him. Fred was flown to the hospital by helicopter with the impact of the crash leaving the entire left side of his body completely destroyed.

Mitch and I were escorted through the chaos of nurses and doctors to where Fred lay on a gurney. The doctor had tried to prepare us for what we were about to see, but no words, tone, or description could possibly have conveyed the situation.

Fred's limp body was lying on a gurney, a pool of blood gathering beneath him. The sound of a groan emerged from Fred as he saw me standing there with Mitch. "He can't talk," the doctor warned. The impact had crushed Fred's palate, leaving him unable to speak. I clutched Mitch's hand even harder.

"We have to take him to X-Ray," a nurse in scrubs said as they wheeled him away. Fred slowly lifted his good hand into the air, giving me the thumbs up sign, as if to say everything was going to be okay.

How I wished I could believe him.

The X-ray results revealed that although Fred's visible injuries were terrible, the non-visible internal ones were far more serious. The crash had all but destroyed him—inside and out. All we could do was wait.

For the next twelve days, I sat diligently at Fred's bedside, willing him to stay alive. Although he couldn't talk, he could still blink his eyes or lift his finger, so I knew that he could hear me. I remember one time he lifted his good hand in the air, motioning rapidly. "Sweetheart, I don't know what you're trying to say," I told him gently. He reluctantly put down his hand.

Mitch and Karen spent every day with me at the hospital, hoping for a miracle while other family members and friends came and went—many of them hopelessly sobbing in the hallway.

Yet, I was so certain Fred was coming home that I had already started planning how to build ramps outside the condo for his wheelchair. To me, there was never a question about whether or not he would be coming home.

I later learned that the drunk driver had a previous conviction for drunk driving and was out of custody on probation for the prior offense. He was the owner of a local bar and had been there drinking since early that fateful morning.

Fred had gone to the golf course just a few minutes away and hit a couple buckets of practice balls. He began the short drive home around 1:00 p.m.

The drunk driver was heading toward Fred from the opposite direction and had hit the center curb at full speed, causing his car to become airborne. There was nothing Fred could have done as the other vehicle landed directly on top of his Toyota, crushing it completely.

Eyewitnesses told police that when they checked on the drunk driver still behind the wheel of the car all he said was, "Shit happens."

Hearing that was like a gut punch. *What kind of vile human being could say such a thing?*

For those twelve days I was practically living at the hospital, staying long past the posted visiting hours. One night Mitch, Karen, and I decided to take a short break from our bedside watch and went to a nearby Asian restaurant for dinner. Even though we were apart, my thoughts were focused on Fred. He had survived a year in Korea and never let his ongoing battle with MS get him down. I couldn't even begin to imagine my strong sixty-year-old husband gone. I prayed he would conquer this as well.

Arriving back at the hospital, the ICU doctor pulled me aside before I reached Fred's hospital bed. He said that while we were gone Fred's condition had worsened and they had to put him into a medically induced coma. Fred could no longer move a finger, not an eyelash, nothing.

With Fred comatose I no longer had any way of knowing whether he could hear me or not. I could have killed the doctor. "How could you have done that without my permission?" I screamed at him. "How could you do that without my being here?"

I think that's why they did it, because I was gone. It was something that had to be done because Fred was fighting the breathing machine. They had turned it all the way up to 100 percent, and he was still fighting it, so I'm certain it was necessary. But I should have been involved. I never had the chance to say goodbye.

The doctors told me that I could still try to talk to him. "Maybe he can hear you," they said.

Maybe.

My rose-colored glasses fell off at that point. All of my optimism drained out of my body and the harsh reality of how this was going to end had begun to seep in.

May 22nd.

As I arrived home after another exhausting day at the hospital, I could hear the sound of my telephone ringing when I opened the door. I hurried across the room to pick up the receiver. The hospital was calling to tell me that Fred had suffered a Code Blue. He had gone into cardiac arrest, and the doctors were trying to resuscitate him.

I rushed back to the hospital where I saw Fred lying in his bed while the doctors and nurses in the room were all laughing and joking around—oblivious to the man lying there barely clinging to life. My husband. My rock.

I was furious. "What is wrong with you?" I screamed at them. "Have a little respect!" Immediately they dispersed, leaving me and my husband alone.

I leaned over and kissed Fred on the cheek. I knew what I had to do. I whispered in his ear, "I love you, sweetheart, and if you need to go, I'll be okay."

I turned away for a moment and when I turned back my husband was gone. He had heard me after all. Fred just needed my permission to go.

I stayed with him for a long time after he died. I couldn't leave. How does one say a final goodbye to a husband of thirty-eight years?

Fred and I had a special song that we would sing to each other since we were young—"Two Sleepy People." The song tells of a couple in love, who stay up together until dawn because they do not want to say good night and part.

And so, I quietly began to sing our special song to him. I would have stayed by his side all night, but Mitch and Karen finally had to drag me away.

In the days that followed, a myriad of random memories swirled in my head.

I thought about the day of the crash. Before leaving the condo to go to the art show, I stopped by Fred's desk to say goodbye, giving him a quick kiss on his bald head as he shuffled bills and papers, not knowing that it would be our last kiss.

I thought about Fred lying in his hospital bed, unable to speak to me and motioning in the air with his right hand. Sadly, I had to tell him I didn't understand. It dawned on me then that he had been gesturing to write. What did Fred want to say? His final attempt at communication was now lost to me forever.

I thought about how just two nights before the car crash, Fred had arranged a wonderful celebration for my fifty-sixth birthday. I shared this special occasion with my son, Mitch, who had been born twenty-six years earlier on the same day. The celebration was at Mitch's favorite sushi restaurant, Crazy Fish on Pico Boulevard in Los Angeles, and I was elated to see my longtime friends and family there—all of us together, enjoying the celebration of life.

Fred wasn't known for his gift-giving but this time he had gone out of his way, showering me with luxuries I had been salivating over for months: a crystal ice bucket and crystal clock. It was so thoughtful—I was completely bowled over! Arranging the lavish party, the gifts, the affection … it was all so out of character. Was something telling him that time was running out? Did he sense that it would be the last time to show his appreciation for me?

Meanwhile, I had to cope with what this drunk driver had done to my family and to me. Not only was Fred my husband, he was a father, a grandfather, and a friend to many. So many lives were ruined the day that this drunk driver, this monster, decided to get behind the wheel intoxicated.

I did my best to press on, beginning with Fred's funeral arrangements. I had not prepared in any way for this. Who would have, when the deceased was only 60 years old?

Fred was not what you would call a religious man, and he had made it clear that he wanted to be cremated. I knew he would never have wanted a religious funeral, but he would have wanted to have a big party to celebrate his life.

My family and I chartered a boat to scatter Fred's remains into the ocean. He loved the ocean. Karen, Mitch, and I each took turns placing a hand into the square wooden box, scooping out the soft gray ashes—all that was left of Fred. We watched the particles blow briefly into the wind and drift down until they were embraced by the blue waves. Fred's final resting place.

Afterward, we returned home where friends and family members were awaiting us. It was the party Fred would have wanted, with good friends and good food. I was the consummate hostess, entertaining the guests and making them all feel at ease and unburdened by the real reason we were gathered. "Sit down,

Chickie," a couple of guests said—but I couldn't. They didn't understand that in order to keep it together I needed to keep moving.

Everyone shared their memories and stories of Fred. There was laughter and more than a few tears were shed. Only after everyone had left and I was alone, did I finally allow myself to feel my great loss. I gave in to my grief and broke down in tears.

Days later I was still finding tiny particles of cremation dust under my fingernails. I felt that Fred was still clinging to me. A strange comfort.

Finding the emotional strength to sit down at my desk to work weeks later was difficult, although having my company to turn to was a much-needed distraction. I knew I needed it just as much as it needed me.

Despite wanting to lie down in bed and not face having to post another bail-bond, I longed to work—to try to find some way to get my life back on track.

"Chickie's Bail Bonds, may I help you?"

My voice was a far cry from its usual exuberance. It was the first business call I had answered since Fred's crash.

The woman on the phone timidly asked me if I would be able to bail out her husband John who was being held at the Manhattan Beach Jail. Instinctively I reached for my yellow pad to jot down the particulars. "What's the charge?" I asked.

"He's been arrested for drunk driving."

I couldn't believe it. My stomach lurched as a wave of emotions flooded through my body—pain, sorrow, and heart-wrenching loss. The image of my husband's body on a gurney flashed in my mind's eye, the image I was desperately trying to erase from my memory.

I can't do this. I can't help this person. Part of me wanted to hang up the phone but as I got ahold of myself another side of me took over.

I was committed to the law that an innocent person not remain in custody, and an arrestee is innocent until declared guilty by a judge. That was my pledge when I became a bail-bond agent. It was my responsibility and my obligation. Despite my heavy, sorrow-filled heart I drove to the jail.

John, a somewhat disheveled young man, listened intently as I explained the terms of his release. "The bond I have posted allows you to remain free until your case is over as long as you make all of your court appearances. If you fail to do so, and we cannot find you, the deed of trust you have signed allows me to foreclose on your home in order to pay the court the amount of your bail."

He nodded, assuring me that he fully understood.

I don't usually inject my personal experience into my business but in this instance, I felt compelled to. I told John in a somber tone, "My husband was recently killed by a drunk driver. It has changed my life. My children and grandchildren lost their wonderful father and grandfather. I'll never forget what it was like to see him on that bloody gurney and what we endured after."

Tears welled up in my client's eyes as he looked down at the table between us, avoiding my stare and clearly ashamed of what he had done. "I'm so sorry," he said, choking back tears. "I promise never to drink and drive again." His anguish was sincere. We hugged.

Driving home from the jail I didn't know if John would be able to keep his promise, but I like to think that relating my story had created a definite possibility—that Fred's tragic end had meaning and purpose and that he did not suffer in vain. *Zikhrono livrakha. May his memory be a blessing.*

That night in bed I stared at the empty space next to me. I had never had my own bed before. I had gone from my mother's bed to Fred's bed and now I was alone. My mother had always said that the worst thing in life was to be alone. She ended up alone. Was this to be my fate as well? Would I ever be able to get into bed without thinking of Fred?

I don't believe there are coincidences in life. The fact that my husband was killed by a drunk driver and that the first bond I wrote when I went back to work was for a drunk driver compels me to think it must have been Fred, sending me a sign. In an odd way it brought me some closure with Fred's death.

-11-

CHICKIE BECOMES A VICTIM

Three armed police officers had ransacked my home! For over an hour they rummaged, prodded, smashed, and pillaged until my condo was turned upside down. My business office upstairs was unrecognizable.

Mary, my very pregnant secretary, had hobbled down the staircase at the incessant banging on my condo door. "POLICE—OPEN THE DOOR!" they shouted many times, loud enough for all my neighbors to hear.

It began at exactly 9 a.m. when I was out of the office handling a case in downtown Los Angeles, concerned as my calls to the office went unanswered.

Three officers, guns drawn, ordered Mary to sit on my dining room chair, shouting, "Do not move!" while pointing their guns at her face.

Two of the officers attacked my living room, overturning furniture, and carelessly tossing pillows onto the floor. The indoor plants were all overturned as though they had been searched—but for what?

The third officer ran up the stairs and attacked my office. He ransacked my files, flinging them carelessly onto the floor as he moved onto the next area to ravage. The filing cabinets were emptied. All files that appeared financial in nature were boxed for transport, leaving the rest in shambles.

My bedroom was not impervious to the assault. My bed was torn apart, the mattress and pillows tossed and turned. My clothes closet was ransacked. Clothing belonging to my late husband whose ashes I had recently sprinkled into the ocean was thrown on my bed in disrespect.

I had been accused of the heinous act of concealing felonious funds, and of committing the much larger crime of lying in court—misrepresenting facts while under oath.

Without even being told, I knew exactly who had sent the police officers.

Arnold Kleinberg, Bakersfield District Attorney

Arnold was the DA in whose case I had recently been involved—an illegal immigrant who had been arrested for smuggling drugs.

Arnold was a miserable man, and Bakersfield was the last place that he wanted to be. The last place anyone would want to be. In the early 1990s, Bakersfield was referred to as the "armpit of California courts." The area was a barren land sparsely surrounded with orange orchards, where a big night on the town meant going to McDonalds or a disreputable bar, of which there were many.

Arnold Kleinberg's Los Angeles law practice had collapsed, along with his ten-year marriage—to his third wife. Life certainly wasn't going the way he had envisioned. "Beggars can't be choosers," he would quip when asked about his new position as Bakersfield's DA.

During the case, Arnold felt that I had somehow pulled one over on him in the courtroom after he unsuccessfully tried to prevent my client from being released on bail.

In cases where drugs are concerned, the state court will often require what is called a 1275 hearing. It is the agent's responsibility to prove to the court that all of the premium, the cash paid for the posting of the bond and the collateral that can be turned into cash should a defendant flee and the court have to be paid, are not associated with the defendant and are not from felonious funds. I had worked hard preparing the documentation to prove these facts and was kept on the stand answering question after question about my work product, a ridiculous amount of time.

It didn't make any sense. Not only was I innocent of these allegations, but I found the whole thing to be incredibly insulting. I took great pride in upholding the law and had worked diligently at earning and maintaining an excellent reputation in the bail-bond industry and the courts. Arnold Kleinberg clearly had a personal vendetta.

The police officers made one final sweep of my condo and then briskly marched out the door, their arms piled high with boxes teetering on top of each other.

After the police left, Mary was finally able to page me. I was on my way home from the court having no idea what was awaiting me.

Seeing my condo in total disarray was an absolute horror. My home, my sanctuary, now lay before me in complete chaos. My first thought was that we had been robbed. "What happened?" I asked Mary, who was still shaking like a leaf. She could barely stammer out the words. "The police were here."

Residual shards of glass crunched under my feet as I wandered from room to room, following the smudge of dirty footsteps, the scuff marks on the wall, the trail of broken dishes. Each one a lingering shadow of what had just transpired.

I couldn't begin to fathom how I was going to clean up the mess. Incredulously, I picked up a plant holder that had been dumped out. *Did they really think I was hiding something in the soil?*

Mary told me what happened and began sweeping up pieces of broken records that were strewn about, records that Fred and I had collected over our decades together. It had been less than a month since Fred's death and I was still putting the pieces of my life back together, trying to process the deep and eternal void of him being gone. I clenched my jaw, refusing to give in to feelings of despair or defeat. But when I walked into my bedroom and saw my late husband's clothes tossed all over the bed, I had serious trouble fighting back tears.

The officers had rummaged through all of my possessions in search of cash they suspected I had been hiding. I saw that they had tipped my jewelry box over and my necklaces and rings had spilled onto the floor—my box of treasures.

I don't believe in buying jewelry for myself. Jewelry has to be sentimental. Someone has to have given it to me so that I can look at it and say, "Wow, you know who gave that to me?" and then I can always remember that special moment in time.

These weren't just my things; these were mementos—memories of a lifetime. My personal belongings, my clothing, everything. All of it had been groped, pawed, desecrated—and all without my knowledge or permission. These police officers had invaded my life. Complete strangers. I had become an object of prey in the one place considered a refuge from attack by predators—my home. To them, I was no more than a rabbit to a fox. This was the kind of thing that innocent defendants were forced to go through when real, actual evidence was not enough and the prosecutor was hell-bent on a conviction.

Mary was still in shock, so I sent her home. She was due any day. As she collected her things she pointed upstairs, "They took your files."

I immediately darted up the stairs. Entering my home office was the worst part of this devastating experience. My office was the heart of my home, and they had stolen the life blood of Chickie's Bail Bonds. Those files were the source of my livelihood; they held confidential information on all of my current and past cases as well as all my financial records. Without those files, it would be impossible for me to run my business. And Arnold knew it.

After the death of my husband, I poured myself into my business. A welcome distraction. It became my other half. The police officers didn't just take my files—they took a piece of me. A piece I didn't know if I could get back. I felt violated.

I had seen this type of thing play before with innocent

defendants. I was quite familiar with the playbook. I just never thought it would happen to me.

Once I became involved in the criminal justice system, I became very much aware that the word "fair" was not always part of the vocabulary any more than the word "justice."

Over the years, I've gotten to know a multitude of prosecuting attorneys, defense attorneys, and judges. We would like to think of all prosecutors as unbiased, believing they are there to uphold the law and seek justice against anyone who commits a crime. There are many men and women who fit the bill, but there are also those whose only desire is to win and punish the accused—regardless the certainty of guilt. These I would categorize as "little Caesars," whose egos and need for power cloud their sense of fair play and justice.

There was a case that stands out in my mind involving a young, female prosecutor. She was completely unwilling to lose. My client had been arrested, and his family was trying to get him released on bail. But he remained in custody, hearing after hearing, while the prosecutor demanded more and more documentation proving that the funds being used for his bond were "clean" and not the profits from his alleged nefarious activities.

Making things even more difficult in this case was that all my client's family and friends—as well as assets—were in Chicago. Month after month his family would fly to Los Angeles with new documentation in hand only to hear that something else was needed. After several such frustrating experiences they gave up. My client was denied bail and forced to remain in custody waiting for his day in court, often months if not years, from the date of arrest.

Prosecutors are not always known for their fairness. Once they decide to prosecute a person for a crime, their focus is to stop at nothing until they win. Unfortunately, their job sometimes shifts from seeking the truth to seeking success—to put the defendant away.

What goes on in the courtroom is a dance. It's a dance between the prosecution and the defense. The prosecuting attorney is dancing with the defense attorney. And they are dancing around the courtroom, each attempting to lead, each attempting to prove their position.

The defense attorney has taken an oath that he will do the best that he can for his client—which could mean not necessarily bending the truth, but perhaps not revealing all of the facts.

In a criminal case, the burden of proof is on the prosecution. The prosecutor has the burden of proof to show that the defendant is guilty. They must convince the jury beyond a reasonable doubt that the defendant committed the crime of which they are accused.

Until this case I had considered myself an innocent player in the game.

<hr>

Earlier in the year, I had responded to a call from an attorney who asked me to become involved in a Bakersfield court case where a young, illegal immigrant man, Manuel Gutierrez Jr., had been arrested on a drug charge with a bail of $325,000.

The collateral and premium for the bond were to be taken care of by Mr. and Mrs. Robinson who were licensed realtors from the Glendale area of Los Angeles. By all accounts the married couple were reputable members of the community. They assured me that the accused's uncle Rafael was a particularly good client and they were merely helping their client by agreeing to be responsible for his nephew's bond.

I felt more comfortable when the persons responsible for a bond were family or close friends of the defendant, but the Robinsons had sufficient equity in three pieces of real estate and had no criminal record or financial ties to the defendant, which qualified them as ideal indemnitors.

As was common with drug cases, the court demanded a 1275

bail hearing, where all equities (premium as well as collateral) being used in conjunction with the bail be scrutinized by the district attorney and approved by the court before bail can be posted and the defendant released pending trial.

With the substantial paperwork in hand necessary to prove that the bond's collateral and funds were legitimate, the Robinsons and I joined the defense attorney early one morning at the Bakersfield County Courthouse. This was all routine and I was fully prepared.

Most bail hearings were fairly short; I was asked a few questions under oath and showed a few documents. I remember a similar case in downtown Los Angeles where the prosecuting attorney refused to even look at my paperwork as soon as he saw that I was the posting bail agent. I had prepared a beautiful file of substantiating documents, but he merely waived me on as soon as he saw the name Chickie's Bail Bonds … that was my reputation.

As the proceedings began and I was called to the stand, it became evident that something was amiss. An uneasy feeling began to grow. This was not just some regular bail hearing. They were going after ME!

I was required to endure days of intense questioning by the district attorney about every aspect of the bond and every detail of my work product. Never before had my work and integrity been so deeply challenged. Accusations flew at me while I tried to maintain my composure. Defending myself, time and again, I was stunned. I was a respected bail agent and had been for six years and yet they were treating me as if I was a criminal. As if I had done something illegal. The shoe was on the other foot and, boy, did it pinch. Obviously, Bakersfield District Attorney Arnold Kleinberg did not want this defendant out on bail!

Eventually, the judge concluded that I had provided all of the necessary documentation, impeccably prepared, and there was no excuse for keeping the defendant in custody. At long last, after four days of being grilled on the stand by the unrelenting district attorney, the court declared I could finally post the bond.

District Attorney Kleinberg was quite unhappy, to say the least. But he had to accept the judge's decision and Gutierrez was released from custody.

With my premium and the collateral for the bond secure, I was a happy camper. I felt certain that the most difficult part of this case was behind me. But some cases are cursed from the start. That certainly was the situation here.

When a very official-looking envelope appeared in the mail a month later I braced for what was lurking inside. Official-looking envelopes were never a good thing. I opened it. Staring me straight in the face were the dreaded words: FORFEITURE NOTICE.

Manuel Gutierrez Jr. did the unthinkable and failed to make his obligatory first court appearance. The court declared the bail forfeited, meaning that I had 180 days to bring him back or suffer the consequences. I would be on the hook for the full $325,000—the bond amount.

Time was ticking. I immediately contacted the Robinsons who said Manuel's uncle Rafael had just told them that Manuel had returned to Mexico after his release. The Robinsons were very apologetic, denying any kind of collusion with Uncle Rafael who insisted he had not heard anything further from Manuel—he had simply disappeared into Mexico.

My heart sank. Things had just gotten even more complicated. The Robinsons would be required to come up with the $325,000 if we could not bring Manuel back to face his charges.

Flipping through my rolodex, I suggested the next step should be hiring a professional bounty hunter to find Manuel and bring him back to the United States. My finger hovered over an index card with several bounty hunters' names, just waiting for the Robinsons to give me the go ahead. "That would just be a waste of money," they said. Rafael had assured them that Manuel would have buried himself deep into Mexico where he would never be found.

I countered, telling them that my bounty hunters were excellent and that it was their best chance at recovering the large sum of money they were about to lose. But the Robinsons were convinced that any and all efforts to locate Manuel would be futile.

This left me with only one choice—to foreclose on their properties. Upon hearing this, the Robinsons implored me not to. They said they would do anything—that foreclosing on their properties would destroy them financially. The Robinsons suggested that they could take out loans on the properties in order to pay the court. "Please," they begged.

I could have ended the whole thing right there and arranged the foreclosures, but their pleas resonated with me. I couldn't live with the knowledge of ruining this family's livelihood. I wanted to do the right thing—in this case, polishing up my rose-colored glasses, listening to my heart instead of my head.

Although somewhat dubious, I always put my clients' needs first and agreed to wait for the loans to come through. These were respectable members of the Glendale community. I convinced myself I had nothing to fear.

Shortly thereafter, the district attorney's investigator called me. "Did you foreclose on the properties?" he asked haughtily.

If they weren't going to get their conviction, they were assuredly going to get their $325,000. I explained that I didn't have any intention of foreclosing on the properties because the Robinsons were obtaining loans against them in order to pay the forfeiture. Apparently, this was unheard of—a bail agent with a heart.

The investigator was instantly annoyed. He had a strange tone to his voice—suspicious—as if he didn't believe me. Meanwhile, I was patting myself on the back for considering the needs of my client.

Two days later, the search warrant was executed on my condo. Not only did the police search my home, they simultaneously did the same to the Robinsons' home, their office, and the escrow office they used. At nine o'clock sharp, the police had invaded all four locations.

I knew that this was Arnold Kleinberg's way of getting even

with me for "putting one over on him"—his view of what had happened in the courtroom. It didn't matter to the district attorney that there was not one shred of evidence to support his suspicions. They found nothing remotely incriminating in my home or office, or in any of the Robinsons' locations either.

Once the searches were complete and the district attorney had backed off, the Robinsons gave me the $100,000 they had borrowed against one of their properties, which I forwarded to the court as a first payment. They were $225,000 short of the full amount required to avoid foreclosure, but the Robinsons assured me that the funds would be available soon. I wanted to believe them, not considering why they wouldn't have obtained loans on all three properties for the full amount of $325,000 instead of $100,000 on one.

As the 180 day deadline was approaching rapidly, the date when the $225,000 would be due, the Robinsons asserted that there was no more money to be had, suggesting I foreclose on their properties. At least I had that option to avoid having to cover the balance myself. However, when I attempted to foreclose, I was informed that the Robinsons had stopped making mortgage payments on their properties months ago and that the real estate which was at one time more than sufficient to cover the bond was now worthless. To add insult to injury, the Robinsons then declared bankruptcy.

It was clear. I had been duped. The district attorney was right to be mistrustful of the people involved in this case.

Months went by without an apology from the District Attorney's office for the terrible break-in of my home or for demand for the balance of the payment. I held my breath, hoping the $100,000 they had received would satisfy my indebtedness, and knowing that if the court did not make demand for the balance timely, they would lose jurisdiction, and therefore, the ability to do so.

Unfortunately, I received a most dreadful call from the same investigator with whom I had spoken previously. He informed me that the balance of $225,000 was due forthwith, meaning right now!

It was an expensive lesson for me. Nearly a quarter of a million dollars out of my pocket and right into the Bakersfield coffers. Sometimes trying to do good in an industry wrought with bad people can have devastating consequences.

When I tried to pursue civil action against the Robinsons, I wound up shelling out even more money for legal expenses. And, of course, that all proved fruitless. Some cases are cursed from the start until the very end.

The court had been financially satisfied when they received the $325,000, the full amount of the bond I had posted. But what about me? The indignity, the embarrassment, to say nothing of the frightful mess they made of my personal property and my office? Wasn't I entitled to at least an apology? I am still waiting.

-12-

WANTING WHAT SHE COULDN'T HAVE

When I told my date that I just had to make a quick stop before going out for dinner, he had no idea that I meant the Beverly Hills Jail.

I was dressed to the nines for my evening out with Dr. Bob. We had reservations at a charming restaurant overlooking the water, but when a client was waiting in custody, the words "later" and "tomorrow" didn't exist.

The year was 1993 and it was my third date with Dr. Robert Berkowitz. Bob was handsome with strong, broad shoulders and always sporting a hat. As I slid into the passenger seat of his Cadillac I explained where exactly the "quick stop" was. He raised an eyebrow, "We're driving to the jail?"

Affable and agreeable, he was the opposite of Fred. Bob happily obliged, following my directions across town to the Beverly Hills Jail.

Gayle Skinner had been arrested for shoplifting at Neiman Marcus in Beverly Hills and she was waiting for me to bail her out. Walking through the jail, Bob's eyes widened as he craned his neck around to drink it all in. This was all so commonplace for me, but I could tell he was shell-shocked. Obviously, he had not set foot in a jail before.

Posting a bond is a relatively quick procedure, especially for an experienced bail agent. I had the paperwork completed and was ready to post the bond on arrival. Bob sat on one of the lobby chairs while I went up to the desk and handed in my paperwork which would then be passed along to the jailer to be processed.

Bob didn't have very much to say while we waited for Gayle to come out. He just sat there digesting the moment. Bob knew what I did for a living, but this was his first experience personally witnessing it. I thought he might be appalled or upset that I had taken him to jail—but he wasn't. He was intrigued.

After Fred's passing, I thought my life was over. I was 56 years old and I had never felt more alone in my life. The world travels two by two and I was just one. The thought occurred to me that if I should disappear, who would even know or care? My children were grown with lives of their own. What did I have? Nothing.

I didn't want to follow the same path as my mother and live the rest of my life alone. At the same time, I was reluctant to rush into a relationship the way I did with Fred.

Little girls grow up fantasizing themselves as Cinderella, imagining being whisked away by the handsome prince to live happily ever after in his glorious castle. I was no different.

Even in my marriage, I still wished for a great romance. At the ripe old age of 23, I saw the movie musical *South Pacific*, and I was captivated by the words of my favorite song, "Some Enchanted Evening." The thought of my eyes locking with a stranger across a crowded room and instantly knowing it was true love, sounded perfect to me.

How utterly romantic! Of course, I knew it was only a fantasy, that it could never come true. There was no time for romance in my life when I went to work every day—only part-time as Fred insisted—as long as I still managed to pull the weeds in the garden he was so proud of.

And yet I would see other couples that were engrossed with each other. Couples of all ages walking, holding hands. Fred and I were young and in love, weren't we? Then why did I feel so alone? I tried a number of times to express to him what I felt was missing from our marriage but to no avail. I didn't know how to make Fred see life as I saw it. As far as he was concerned our relationship was fine. These conversations eventually prompted Fred to ask his health professional for advice, saying his wife wanted romance in our lives. His doctor's advice was to take me out to dinner. Which Fred did. Once.

Fred and I had had a strong connection based on years of marriage and love for each other. Looking back on our relationship I knew that my early fantasies of romance were just that—fantasies of a young woman thrust early in life into adulthood. Now I could appreciate what I had. Now, when it was too late.

With Fred gone a vast emptiness constantly enveloped me. The overwhelming sorrow from his death had torn open a wound so deep that no nurse or doctor could ever stitch it closed. A Band-Aid would have to suffice.

The first Band-Aid came in the form of Dean Williams, the owner of Dolores's restaurant. We had known each other for years, since I had so frequently used his restaurant as my office. Dean's fiancé had just broken up with him and he was devastated.

At Fred's funeral he approached me and patted me on the shoulder trying to comfort me. "Oh, Chickie, don't worry. We'll go to the movies," he said. Those were his exact words! As if that was going to make me feel better.

Then I thought about my friend Bernice. Even though she had been divorced for years, she always had a handsome man to escort her to weddings and Bar Mitzvahs. She attended Fred's funeral with "Big Al" who was down on his luck and happy to escort her around.

No sex, no heavy emotions. Just friendship. It seemed it worked for her.

Within a week Dean called and invited me out to the movies. "Just as friends." I accepted. After all, what could it hurt? We went out a couple of times, and I discovered that Dean's companionship helped in taking my mind off my loss—even if it was just temporarily. After a while I actually began looking forward to our outings.

When Dean's fiancé returned, Dean gave me the tickets he had purchased for us to see Jackie Mason. I took Mitch, and we had a great time! Later I was happy to hear that Dean married his fiancé. Band Aid Number One bit the dust!

At about the same time, Bernice called to let me know that Big Al said he would be happy to be my "escort" as he had been for years for her.

When Big Al called to let me know he was available, "Band Aid Number Two" was created.

Al and I would occasionally go out together. It was nice but we were really just keeping each other company. I was especially grateful for Al when the holidays came around, the first of the hurdles to be overcome without my husband of 38 years.

Al suggested we throw a New Year's Eve party and invite some of his friends as well as some of mine. The party was a big success. Although being surrounded by couples kissing at midnight, I couldn't help yearning for someone to love.

Then came Band Aid Number Three: a most unlikely match.

When I was 19—married to Fred with a new baby—our downstairs neighbors, Sylvia and Murray, became our very good friends. Their cousin Seymour stopped by our apartment one day to say hello. He was tall, thin, and handsome with a head of thick, lustrous hair. He invited Fred and me to a party that he and his wife were having at their home in San Marino. The night of the party he taught me how to drink tequila with lemon and salt—an accomplishment for a non-drinker—and made me feel like a beautiful woman, not just a housewife with a new baby.

When Seymour found out that I was recently widowed, he got my phone number from his cousin Sylvia and reached out to me. He needed a female on his arm for a fancy event. Seymour was no longer married. He had been through a few wives and many girlfriends but was officially unattached. I agreed, excited to see the handsome, jubilant man I once knew.

But that man never arrived. The young, slender, good-looking Seymour from my youth was gone and in his place was an old, fat, and completely bald Seymour.

His disposition had also completely changed. Years of failed relationships and the pitfalls of life had slowly chipped away at him, leaving a cynical and bitter shell of a man. Seymour wanted me in his life, and I was intolerably lonely enough to agree, enjoying the attention although from a pathetic individual. As much as I enjoyed going out to dinner to fancy restaurants, I often felt like crawling under the table as Seymour carried on with the waitress about how important it was that the food be prepared without a drop of any fat, no oil etc., of any kind. As he sat there, almost a hundred pounds overweight, who did he think he was fooling? The cache of boxes of chocolate bars in his kitchen confirmed all my negative thoughts.

I spent time with Seymour for about six months—nothing sexual. When my friends saw us together, they were appalled. They were looking at the current Seymour and not the younger version I was still desperately clinging to in my mind's eye.

Seymour's personality began to grate on me. He would brag about how often he had visited Israel. "You haven't been to Israel?" he would say to me with mock surprise. "I've been eight times! You've never been once?"

After months of this, Seymour decided that I needed to go to Israel and that he was going to take me. He was adamant that I go. I agreed with the caveat that my good friends Linda and Ron come along and so off the four of us went.

What a thrill it was! From the moment we landed, riding in a cab down boulevards with street signs written in unmistakable Hebrew brought tears to my eyes. A language I could not understand but loved. It was an all-expense paid trip for me. Unfortunately, Linda, Ron, and I had to do everything Seymour wanted to do and go wherever Seymour wanted. His negative outlook was spoiling the whole trip, like a rain cloud following us around. Since Seymour had the car and did the driving, he would take us to one of the many wonderful sights of Israel, which he would point out as his car sped on to the next site, which we would also not have a moment to enjoy!

When we'd finally had enough of Seymour and his unpleasant ways, I joined Linda and Ron in moving from Herzliya to Tel Aviv—away from Seymour—though I did invite him to join us, saying I would pay for the Tel Aviv Hotel. His haughty response was, "I cannot be bought." To which I responded, "Goodbye, Seymour."

Each day of exploring with Linda and Ron I kvelled at the wonders of this tiny country. It was magical being there.

It was late, around 10 p.m., as I sat with Linda and Ron in the bustling lobby bar of the Dan Hotel in Tel Aviv. Lively noise filled the entire space: drinks clinking, plates clattering, and people from all over the world chatting in a variety of different languages.

Suddenly, for no reason I can imagine, I stood up in time to see a tall handsome stranger coming through the doorway. He wore a straw hat, had a camera around his neck, and a tour guide in his pocket. Completely out of character, I suddenly pointed in his direction and let out a very loud, "OH LOOK—THAT MAN'S A TOURIST!" Obviously, a ridiculous remark with the entire hotel occupied by tourists. A big smile lit up his face, and he ambled over and we introduced ourselves. He seemed delighted to learn that we lived in close proximity in Los Angeles and then entered into an animated conversation with my friend Ron about archeological digs. When I realized how late it was, I announced that my cousin would be waiting downstairs to take us to dinner and we had to leave. But before doing so, I pulled the tour guide from his pocket and wrote my name and room number on it, shoved it back in his pocket, and off the three of us went.

"Chickie, baby…" a husky voice said when I answered my hotel phone the following morning at 9:15. My heart began to flutter. *It was him.*

Talk about an opening line.

Bob and I arranged to go to dinner that evening with Linda and Ron at a nearby restaurant.

Linda and I ran around like schoolgirls that afternoon, getting our hair and nails done in anticipation of the evening, although neither of us could remember the name of the handsome stranger.

As we headed out to dinner that night, all four of us crammed into one taxi. Ron gave Bob the third degree, questioning him, being protective of me, making sure Bob wasn't a mass murderer or anything nefarious. Bob just laughed, taking it all in stride.

After the taxi dropped us off, we entered the restaurant and were shown to a table. As Bob and I sat down, Linda and Ron announced that they didn't like the restaurant and walked out. Bob and I just stared at each other in surprise. I thought it was nice of them to give us some time alone. Clearly, Bob must have passed Ronnie's taxicab inquisition with flying colors. Moreover, I think they were excited that I had finally met someone I was interested in.

Bob was different from anyone I had ever met. He was a total catch. Tall, handsome, and a good conversationist. Perhaps too much of a catch. "Are you married?" was the first question that popped out of my mouth. Tapping his fingers and avoiding my stare, Bob let out a deep sigh. He didn't have to say a word.

Of course he was married. My whole life I had always strived to do the right thing. I was always the good girl, the good wife, the good person. And there I was … on a date with a married man. I considered getting up and leaving, but I didn't. I stayed, rooted in my seat. The attraction between us was impossible to ignore and I couldn't pull myself away from him—nor did I want to. Since he was married, I had no intention of taking this any further with him.

I thought, *We'll just have one nice dinner together and that will be that.*

However, it didn't end at just one dinner. We had such a wonderful time that we decided to spend the next day together, enjoying the city. Bob was always touching me, holding my hand, staring into my eyes. Affection—something I hadn't had in a long time, even with Fred. I thought, *We'll just spend his last day in Israel together and that will be that.*

When I came home to California, I had made the firm decision I was not going to date a married man. Regardless of my desires, I knew that the right thing to do was to stay away.

When Bob called, I agreed to have lunch with him. I felt it was the right thing to do—to see him once and explain how I felt about dating a married man and to tell him I would not be seeing him again. After lunch we sat on a bench overlooking the marina while he explained how he was married "in name only," that he and his wife had had separate bedrooms for ten years. He pleaded with me to reconsider.

Bob was persistent—calling almost daily, never demanding, just lovely conversations, getting to know each other until finally I agreed to go to dinner with him.

For our first dinner date I made a reservation at a local restaurant that I liked. Unfortunately, Bob was extraordinarily uncomfortable because the chairs were just simple wooden chairs that didn't suit his large frame. Nevertheless, we had a lovely time. Bob was the perfect gentleman, holding the door for me, pulling the seat out for me, and touching me any chance he got. With each touch and every glance something stirred deep inside of me—for the first time in a long time I felt alive.

Afterward we went to my place for a night cap. While I prepared our drinks Bob made himself comfortable on my couch. Sitting down next to him I deliberately kept a modest space between us, but the chemistry was palpable. Bob inched closer to me on the couch, his hand caressing my arm as he seductively said, "Well?

When are we going to hug?"

Except he didn't say hug.

I laughed at Bob's question, trying not to be shocked. It seemed logical to ask if we were going to have sex. After mulling it over I decided, *Well... he's a doctor. He's going to know where everything is.*

I knew this relationship would strictly be sexual. It had to be. He was married and I wasn't going to let myself care for him. I could keep my emotions on a shelf and not worry about getting hurt.

Or so I thought.

Waiting at the Beverly Hills Jail with Bob on our "date," it wasn't long before a tearful young woman approached us. It was my client, Gayle. Her face streaked with tears and mascara, her hair a tangled mess—as if she'd been nervously running her fingers through it for hours. Still, she was quite attractive, in her late 20s with crystal blue eyes and dark blond hair—certainly not someone you would expect to be walking out of a jail.

Gale told her story while choking back tears. She was a legal secretary in Beverly Hills. One of her favorite lunchtime pastimes was strolling through posh department stores perusing expensive items she couldn't possibly afford. On that particular day, she had found her way to Neiman Marcus on Wilshire Boulevard.

As she wandered the aisles, Gayle was attracted to a blue silk blouse. Though it was way out of her price range, she decided to try it on. Admiring herself in the mirror wearing this elegant blouse, Gayle felt transformed into a different person—important, rich. A feeling she didn't want to go away.

When she took the silk shirt off, she was overwhelmed with the terrible impulse to keep the blouse. Thinking that nobody would know, Gayle shoved the silk blouse into her purse and, as casually as she could, walked out of the store.

Her victory was short-lived as the plainclothes security men nabbed her, placing her under arrest. She was subsequently incarcerated.

Gayle explained to me that prior to this her record was squeaky clean. Not so much as a parking ticket. "I don't know what came over me!" she cried.

I felt terrible for her. Gayle was despondent—not just because of being arrested, but because there were potential ramifications that would affect her entire life. Her parents would probably view her through different eyes after this. She had always been their golden girl, graduating school with honors and getting into the legal field. They had been so proud of her. She was their only child, and they held her in such high regard.

Then there was her job. Gayle would have to explain to her boss that she had been arrested, with the risk of getting fired looming over her. She might lose everything. All because of one bad judgment call.

Trying to help Gayle come to terms with her situation, I told her that although she made a terrible mistake, it wasn't irreparable. As a first-time offender she would likely just plead guilty to a minimal charge and perhaps pay a small fine with a few weeks of community service. I advised her to stay in close touch with my office so I could provide any appropriate guidance needed. Gayle needed to know that she could count on me during this trying time.

Before I could continue, I was surprised when I saw Bob reach out and hold Gayle's hand. "There there, dear," Bob soothed. "It's going to be all right."

I was awestruck. Bob wasn't just being a spectator he was jumping right in and contributing. He counseled this young lady sympathetically, trying to make her feel better. Almost like a father to a child. She listened intently and in a short time managed to stop crying. He had made a real connection with her. She even started talking to him about her health issues, so he gave her medical advice as well. It was remarkable!

Once Gayle was safely on her way home, Bob and I resumed our date and headed over to the restaurant much later than we originally had anticipated. Excitedly, Bob spoke of our experience that night with Gayle and how he had relished it. "Your job is so fascinating," he said, filled with admiration.

Bob's interest was foreign to me. Fred had never wanted anything to do with my bail bond business, never once asked me about a case. Tentatively, I began to talk about my business and my philosophy of how people aren't necessarily bad, they just make mistakes. Bob hung on my every word, totally enthralled.

He acknowledged that I was an important part of the judicial system. It really gave me a sense of wholeness, that it was okay to be who I am.

He was so easy. It was all so easy. Even though it was only our third date it felt like we'd known each other forever.

Checking his watch, Bob suddenly stood up. "I need to make a quick phone call," he said, as he gave me a peck on the cheek. He walked inside to use the restaurant's phone. My stomach did a small flip-flop. I knew what he was doing. He was calling his wife to report in.

There was an irony to the entire evening. My client, Gayle, wanted something that she couldn't have and acted impulsively, without full regard for the repercussions. Although Bob claimed that his marriage wasn't a marriage at all, technically he belonged to someone else.

Bob wasn't gone long, maybe five minutes. Sitting back down he reached for my hand which was resting on the table. "Now, where were we?"

I smiled one of my wide smiles at him and continued talking as if nothing had happened. As if he hadn't just spoken to his wife and lied about where he was. Pushing away those thoughts, I concluded that the only way I could justify going out with Bob was to tell myself that I was not going to get romantically involved. I fortified my decision to keep myself from falling in love with this man. It was better this way.

But the truth was, like Gayle, I also wanted what I couldn't have.

THE DOCTOR IS IN ... CUSTODY

Of all the crimes that are prosecuted in the criminal justice system, few are considered by the court to be as heinous as threatening a witness. And of all the cases I've worked on, few were as sad as the case of Dr. Harvey White and his wife Gladys.

The Whites were an older couple living in a small rural town outside of Detroit. The judge set bail at an astonishing five million dollars each—a total of ten million dollars for the couple.

My daughter, Karen, had recently moved in with me. She was my firstborn and had always been as straight as an arrow—and there was no bend in that arrow! She had graduated high school early and informed me that there was nothing for her in West Covina where she had grown up. Her friends were involved in drugs and alcohol, which was not her thing. Karen begged me and her father to allow her to go to Israel to work on a kibbutz for a year. It broke my heart to say yes to letting my little girl go off to a strange land, but she promised to come home when the year was up. This, however, was only the beginning of Karen's wanderlust—a path she continued for many years visiting cities all over the world.

I had always wanted Karen to come work with Mitch and me. With her sweet nature and devotion to helping others, I felt she would be a perfect fit. She was never afraid to take on new challenges—I knew she would be a great addition to Chickie's Bail Bonds. When she confessed she wasn't sure what to do next with her life, I suggested she join our company. She was not exactly enthusiastic about the idea.

"There is no way in hell I'm getting involved with criminals," Karen stated adamantly. "I don't want to offend you or anything, Mom … but it's not for me."

Karen knew my point of view on defendants—that they are just people who make stupid mistakes—but she still couldn't wrap her head around the concept. I felt that Dr. White and his wife Gladys were an exemplary case to illustrate the importance of what I was doing. Helping people—not criminals—just people. If I could get Karen to understand what the Whites were going through, perhaps she would see bail from my perspective.

It was an unusual case. Criminal Defense Attorney John Yzurdiaga had called me one morning a few months prior and explained the dire situation of his clients Dr. and Mrs. White, a married couple in their late 60s. His job was to defend the Whites against their criminal charges, but first he had to get them released from custody.

Which is where I came in.

Harvey and Gladys lived in a small town outside of Detroit, Michigan. Harvey was a well-respected oncologist. His wife, a nurse, worked beside him. They were well-known around town and respected members of their church and community. Neither had ever had a run-in with the authorities.

Harvey and Gladys raised a family of seven children, six of whom were married and lived within close proximity. Their youngest son, Anthony, was a bit of a black sheep and had moved to Los Angeles earlier that year to fulfill his lifelong dream of becoming a Hollywood actor.

Anthony had been in Los Angeles a few months when his father received a distressing phone call. Harvey was stunned to learn that his son was calling from jail and had been arrested on a rape charge. Anthony swore to his father that the allegation was not true.

Anthony went on to describe the events that happened the night leading up to the terrible accusation. He had met an attractive young woman at a bar one evening; they both became intoxicated and ended up having sexual intercourse against a fence near the back entrance of the bar. According to Anthony it was consensual. However, the young woman was alleging that it was not and that Anthony had forced himself on her.

Anthony insisted that the woman was lying, that it was a false accusation.

Harvey was beside himself. It didn't sound like Anthony's behavior at all. His son wasn't violent nor was he a liar. Harvey and Gladys prided themselves on raising good Christian children with strict morals.

Believing his son was telling the truth and that the woman was lying, Harvey assured Anthony that he would find a way to clear his name.

Harvey hung up the phone but not before Anthony gave him one piece of information that would ultimately change the course of Dr. Harvey and Gladys' lives—the name of the woman who was making the accusation.

"Janet Jones."

Harvey filled his wife in on their son's grim situation. Gladys was crestfallen, completely unable to believe that her son was being accused of such a terrible crime. In their small, Bible-minded town this kind of thing just didn't happen. The Whites were desperate to help their son but were completely out of their element with no one to turn to. They felt that someone had to talk some sense into this woman who was about to ruin their son's life.

It was at that moment the Whites made a disastrous decision. They obtained Janet Jones' home address and drove cross-country with one intention: to confront their son's accuser face to face.

Harvey and Gladys approached the front door and rang the doorbell. A young woman, blond and attractive, answered the door holding the hand of a little boy, no doubt her son. Harvey and Gladys tried to remain calm amidst their seething fury at what this woman was attempting to do to their son.

"Are you Janet?" Harvey asked. The woman eyeballed them up and down before nodding. "Yes. What do you want?"

Without another word, Harvey thrust a typed note into her hands:

DROP THE CHARGES YOU HAVE BROUGHT AGAINST ANTHONY. WE KNOW WHERE YOU AND YOUR SON LIVE.

Before the Whites had the chance to retrieve the note, Janet spun around and slammed the door in their faces, the note still clutched in her hand.

The Whites drove away, feeling justified in showing Janet they were not taking this lightly. They felt a rape accusation, even if their son was found not guilty, would taint his reputation—especially in their small town where this would spread like wildfire. They were confident they were doing the right thing, to make Janet drop the charges. Of course, they had no intention of harming her or her son.

Meanwhile, as soon as she had slammed the door in their faces, Janet ran to the phone, reporting the incident to the police.

Within just a few blocks, the Whites heard the sound of sirens blaring behind them. They were pulled over by the local police, handcuffed, and charged with the very serious crime of threatening a witness.

The Whites had no idea that they had just committed a criminal act. Witness intimidation, "knowingly and maliciously attempting to prevent a victim from providing testimony in a court proceeding," is a crime taken very seriously by the court system.

The bail schedule lists the majority of crimes where bail can be posted upon arrest and the defendant released from custody without having to appear in court. Serious crimes such as multiple murders and threatening a witness are not listed on the bail schedule. In those cases, the accused must appear before a judge who has the power to set a bail amount, or in especially heinous crimes, refuse to set bail at all, causing the defendant to remain in custody pending the outcome at trial.

The crime of threatening a witness, the crime the Whites had unthinkingly committed, caused Harvey and Gladys to be taken to the Los Angeles County Jail where they would remain until they appeared in court with their attorney who would try to convince the judge to set a reasonable bail and grant the Whites their freedom pending trial.

To the Whites' utter dismay, the Los Angeles County Jail was no smalltown jail. It was in fact the most despicable jail in the state of California, an absolute hellhole. The unwritten rule was: "You don't send a dog to LA County Jail." Hardened criminals had a tough time enduring the conditions, much less two senior citizens totally out of their depth.

At the Whites' first court appearance, their pre-trial hearing, Attorney John Yzurdiaga pled the Whites' case, presenting all of the appropriate arguments before the court. He posited that this was completely out of character for the Whites, who were upstanding members of their community.

I was in court, hoping the bail amount would be within my clients' means. How terribly astonished I was when the judge set bail for the Whites at five million dollars each. This was tantamount to saying "No bail." There was no way these people had the capital necessary to meet that kind of bail amount.

In the courtroom, the feeling from day one was that these people should be released, that they were good people. I'm certain that the judge felt that way as well, but there was good reason why they had to remain in custody.

When it comes to threatening a witness, the principle of "innocent until proven guilty" gets put on indefinite hold. Judges choose to err on the side of caution, the logic being that if a judge were to set bail and the accused followed through on their threat once released, the judge would be held responsible. From a judge's perspective it is better to keep the accused in custody in all cases of threatening a witness.

The Whites were subsequently returned to the dreaded Los Angeles County Jail where they would continue to wither away, waiting for their trial, which could take several months. The Whites, as well as their attorney, John Yzurdiaga, were at their wits' end.

It was apparent that the Whites were just a small-town mother and father who made a huge mistake in an extremely misguided attempt to protect their son. But when you become a parent, you are willing to put your life on the line for your children. You'll do anything to save them.

I'll never forget the time my mother was being so overprotective of me that she wanted to kill my doctor.

At fourteen my doctor told my mother that I needed to have a tonsillectomy. Almost every year I was plagued with throat infections caused by my tonsils. Time after time my mother would take me to see a doctor who would prescribe an antibiotic and I would be fine, until the next time. The doctors assured me and my mother, that a tonsillectomy was a routine surgery—fairly common for children around my age—adding that the recovery would be easy and I would be as good as new.

However, after recovering from the surgery I discovered that I was not "good as new." I had lost the ability to pronounce certain words. My mother was so distressed, that every morning she would awaken me asking me to pronounce my favorite word, "boy," and each morning I would answer, "Poy." Try as I might, I just couldn't pronounce the letter B.

In school I suffered through the class laughing at me when it was my turn to speak. No matter how hard I tried to say some of the words, my mouth just wasn't able to do it. And the harder I tried, the more the class laughed.

My mother was beside herself, thinking that the surgery might have caused permanent damage, berating herself for agreeing to the tonsillectomy. Most of all she was furious with the doctor who had performed the surgery. "I'm going to kill him," she wailed. She spoke of his demise more than once—even going as far as researching where she could buy a gun.

Eventually my ability to pronounce words came back. "Poy" returned to "boy" and all was well. But I truly believe that had my speech not returned to normal my mother absolutely would have bought the gun and done the deed.

Harvey and Gladys White remained incarcerated at the Los Angeles County Jail for months while their attorney scheduled court after court appearance where he pleaded with the judge to set a reasonable bail amount. Time after time, the judge maintained his position—the bail amount stayed at five million dollars each. It appeared the Whites would have to remain in jail until the completion of their trial.

There are times when luck turns things around. Fortunately, this was the case for the Whites. A new judge was sitting on the bench when we arrived at court that day.

I had convinced Karen to come with me and see with her own eyes why bail was so important, that we were really in the business of helping people.

When the defendants were escorted into the courtroom, they looked starkly out of place. Clad in their over-sized orange jumpsuits, both Gladys and Harvey appeared unwell, as if they had aged ten years. Their skin was pallid with dark hollows beneath their eyes—they seemed emaciated. It was clear that the county jail had broken them.

All of the White family had flown into Los Angeles to support Harvey and Gladys—six of their children plus spouses were present in the courtroom hoping for a miracle.

Their son Anthony was missing—still in custody on the rape

charge—the charge that started the Whites down this dark road.

Karen was clearly engrossed in what was happening in the courtroom; seeing Gladys and Harvey in person, obviously misguided parents, certainly not cruel-intentioned; having only tried to do what they thought was best for their son.

Once again, Attorney John Yzurdiaga pled his case, this time before a new judge. Tension mounted, anticipating the court decision. Would this be the judge that finally showed the Whites some mercy?

When the judge announced his verdict, lowering the bail amount to $250,000 each, the gavel struck and there wasn't a dry eye in the courtroom. The emotion was not lost on Karen. I believe it was at that moment she made her decision, deciding to become a part of Chickie's Bail Bonds.

The Whites would finally be allowed to leave the county jail and could spend time with their family as they prepared for their upcoming criminal trial. John Yzurdiaga and I exchanged a few congratulatory words. Thanks to John's perseverance, the bonds releasing Gladys and Harvey from custody could now be posted, granting them their freedom, albeit temporary.

Watching the family's emotional reunion, Karen grasped how important the role of a bail agent is, to ensure that presumed-innocent arrestees were not unnecessarily detained pending trial. How thrilled I was when she turned to me and said, "Okay, I'll come work for you."

The Whites still had a long road ahead of them, facing their own trial plus their son Anthony pleading not guilty to the charge of rape in his upcoming trial. Throughout the entire process he had maintained that it was consensual sex and that he was innocent.

Due to procedural delays, the young man appeared in court time after time where his trial was continued to a later date; either the defense or the prosecution was not prepared.

Dragging out the trial even more, it took two long trials for the jury to arrive at a decision. The first trial was mishandled by the hired private attorney, resulting in a hung jury. In the second trial Anthony was better represented by a public defender—unusual but it happens.

The evidence presented and testimony from several credible witnesses revealed that his sexual encounter with Janet against the fence was indeed consensual. Both Anthony and Janet were intoxicated at the time, and it was not rape! Anthony was at last set free.

When the time came for Harvey and Gladys' trial, I anticipated a guilty verdict with a "slap on the wrist"—possibly a fine or even probation—anything but incarceration.

John Yzurdiaga did an incredible job defending his clients, with a focus on presenting the extenuating circumstances. In a criminal case, extenuating circumstances must be taken into consideration to fully grasp the facts of the case. Depending on the facts presented, extenuating circumstances could lead to a person's actions being viewed as less or more severe. This can create a decreased or increased punishment in a criminal case.

John also called many character witnesses to the stand including Harvey White's 93-year-old father. Each of the witnesses spoke very highly of Harvey and Gladys White—all of which should have held some weight with the court.

Unfortunately, their attorney was faced with a situation where the deck was stacked against them. From my perspective, it didn't help that the judge seemed to be enamored with the female district attorney, hanging onto her every word. As much as those in the criminal justice system try to be impartial, biases and preferential treatment can infringe on the process, whether consciously or subconsciously. All of the evidence John presented to the court seemed to be ignored by the judge.

The jury returned with their verdict. "Guilty."

The word hung heavily in the air. Followed by complete silence.

The Whites visibly flinched as the judge announced that they were being sentenced to two years in prison. This was no slap on the wrist. The older couple would have to pay a significant price for their mistake in judgment.

Harvey was in the men's prison while Gladys did her time in the women's. This took a severe toll on their mental and physical health to the extent that Harvey was diagnosed with late-stage cancer while incarcerated and had to undergo chemo treatment while in prison, sadly unable to have his wife by his side.

Within a week of Harvey's release, he succumbed to the disease.

Although the Whites had suffered deeply from their own situation, they could at least feel some relief that their son had been vindicated.

-14-
PATH TO REDEMPTION

I never considered myself to be the kind of person to have an affair with a married man and yet there I was. This was the type of behavior that was absolutely off limits for a goody two-shoes like me!

Bob and I had been seeing each other for six months, stealing away any chance we could get. We tried to spend as much time together as possible. On weekdays he would telephone me at lunch to say hello, and we would excitedly make plans to meet after work.

One evening I invited Bob to accompany me to a formal charity function where he needed to wear a tuxedo. He smuggled it out of his house and into his car, parking on a busy Beverly Hills street not far from the event. I was half-hysterical watching him wriggle his way into his evening attire while in the front seat of his car, hopefully unnoticed.

Although Bob and his wife were still living under the same roof, they continued to sleep in separate bedrooms and frequently talked about going into arbitration. He lived his life and she lived hers.

What had started as a purely physical relationship had blossomed into more. I suppose it was inevitable. I found happiness and contentment with Bob I'd never known. No matter how much I struggled to fight it, I found I was compromising my beliefs for my heart.

My good friend Charlene Marshall became furious with me

when I told her about Bob. She had also dated "a Bob," not knowing he was married. By the time he confessed he had a wife, it was too late—Charlene was hopelessly in love. She stayed with him waiting for the day that he would leave his wife. She was with him for 20 years; he never left his wife. When he died, she was crushed not to be able to attend his funeral, forced to mourn alone.

Charlene begged me to call it off. "Chickie, how can you do this?" she exclaimed. "Don't you know what I've gone through?"

My relationship with Bob isn't like that, I thought.

Or was it?

I wasn't hooked on Bob. I wasn't deeply and hopelessly in love. In fact, I had never brought up the word "divorce" with him. What if I didn't like him the next day? I didn't want that responsibility.

He never said it, but I knew that Bob loved me from the second we met, telling me with his eyes, his actions, and his constant showering of affection. He never said he loved me out loud … until he did.

It was mid-afternoon on a beautiful September day. We had just finished enjoying lunch at Hamburger Hamlet in Beverly Hills where we had shared a hamburger—even though Bob had said he would never eat ground meat in a restaurant.

On the way back to Bob's car, we stood waiting to cross the street as cars sped all around us. The din of the busy intersection with cars incessantly honking and tires squealing seemed to fade into the background. We were in our own little bubble, as if no one else existed.

Holding my hand as he always did, Bob suddenly turned toward me and said, "I love you."

A rush of blood coursed through my veins into my face as I felt a flush creep over me. My mouth dropped open but no words came out. *Now what do I do?*

I blurted out the first thing that came to mind.

"I want to eat lima beans."

Real life and fantasy life had collided. My time with Bob had been a dream up until this point, but the alarm clock of reality had just buzzed me wide awake. Bereft of speech I simply stood there, blankly staring at him.

Most women dream of hearing those three little words: I love you. But to me it meant that from that moment on things would never be the same. *What do you say to a married man who is telling you he loves you?*

Bob seemed puzzled. "Lima beans?" Certainly not the "L" word he was hoping to hear.

I explained to Bob that for 38 years of marriage I had never eaten lima beans because Fred didn't like lima beans. Whatever Fred wanted me to be, I became—from the time I was 17 until his death.

Bob had broken our unwritten agreement by saying I love you. I didn't want to fall in love with another man, especially a married man. What had I gotten myself into?

The tragedy of Fred's death had completely upended my life. After he died, I would go to the market and walk up and down the aisles with my basket aimlessly. I had no idea what to buy. The once ordinary task of plucking items off the grocery shelves had become daunting. *What did I want for dinner?* I honestly didn't know.

Treading water for two years, I had slowly begun to find my way back toward land—discovering who I was and what I wanted. Chickie's Bail Bonds had given me a sense of self. Having been widowed for two years, I knew who I was and I wasn't about to lose myself again.

I had been left with no choice but to keep my rose-colored glasses polished and to try to make the best of the cards I had been dealt.

One of Chickee's Bail Bonds clients was a pastor whose life

had been drastically altered by a confluence of ill-fated events.

Brazilian-born Pastor Marcos Costa thought he was doing the right thing by getting his commercial trucker's license as a way to supplement his income. His meager earnings from his small church in Massachusetts were not enough to support him and his wife of 22 years.

Marcos' first job as a commercial truck driver was a cross-country trip in a 25-ton double-decker car hauler. Setting out on the open road from the East Coast, Marcos began the long journey.

His final destination was in Los Angeles, California—a city and state he had never visited and fraught with unfamiliar roads and highways. Marcos' GPS indicated that the shortest route was the Angeles Forest Highway, directly through the San Gabriel mountains. Unbeknownst to Marcos, trucks took freeway routes around the rugged mountain range due to the danger involved. The warning signs, however, had for no discernable reason been removed from all of the dangerous mountain roads.

Climbing the side of the mountain, the big rig made its way through the smog, the low visibility obscuring how precariously narrow and steep the route was.

With no way of turning around, Marcos continued to follow the directions on the GPS, taking him down the other side of the San Gabriel mountains along a winding, descending grade of road. He managed to navigate miles and miles of dangerous terrain, but as he reached the bottom of the mountain range and was nearing level ground, the big rig started to pick up speed at an alarming rate. Marcos panicked and slammed on the brakes.

Gaining momentum, the vehicle careened down the hill as smoke began to billow from beneath. Terror overcame Marcos as he realized his brakes were gone and he could not slow the big rig down. Desperately, he scanned the area for a runaway lane but there was none. His vehicle relentlessly barreled toward the bustling retail district of La Cañada Flintridge.

Eyewitnesses reported that they heard the squealing of brakes and the sound of crunching metal as the truck plowed into buildings at the bottom of the hill.

Attempting to negotiate a sharp turn at high velocity, the truck spun out of control into traffic. The rear of the truck jackknifed as it bounced off obstacles and slammed into a red car, pushing it about 200 yards, and killing the driver and his daughter.

The truck then plowed into a bookstore whose patrons had fled. Momentum then carried the truck—loaded with vehicles—into a nail parlor.

A double fatality. With 12 others injured.

Following the crash, Marcos was arrested and booked on one count of gross vehicular manslaughter and one count of felony reckless driving. Bail was set at $200,000.

His wife came to Los Angeles and got hold of us at Chickie's Bail Bonds, desperate to have her husband bailed out. She and Marcos were practically financially destitute; however, they were able to get support from a local Los Angeles church. We posted Marcos' bond and he was released.

Though Marcos was being painted as the villain by many, it couldn't have been further from the truth. He had given so much of his life to his faith and to helping those in need, never expecting anything in return. I couldn't imagine the overwhelming pain he must have felt. For a pastor, believing that God would always provide, how easy it would have been to become disillusioned. Yet his faith in God never wavered.

I was beyond pleased to get Marcos out of custody giving him time to work with his lawyer to prepare his defense, to also spend time with family, and to make necessary preparations for his potential incarceration. The gift of time.

Marcos' crash was a horrific tragedy but not entirely his fault. The guilt should have been shared. It should have gone to the people that had taken down the roadside signs that are normally posted to warn truckers to avoid certain routes. Or to the city that didn't install a runaway lane, or the company that gave a novice truck driver an advanced job like this. Unfortunately, the criminal justice system has a tendency to focus the guilt on one individual.

Less than a year prior, another truck had crashed in the same area. A tractor-trailer from Idaho carrying 78,000 pounds of produce lost its brakes coming down the steep incline, ramming into several cars in a parking lot. One person was hurt in that crash but luckily no one was killed.

A post-crash inspection revealed that five of Marcos's 10 truck brakes either weren't working or were not adjusted correctly. The five working brakes showed signs of overheating or cracking on the pads.

Due to the circumstances, the jury rejected charges of second-degree murder but ultimately convicted Marcos of involuntary manslaughter and he was sentenced to seven years and four months in state prison. With some time already served, and extra credit for good behavior, prosecutors said Costa could be released in about two years.

I remember thinking about this kind soul having to survive in a potentially dangerous environment surrounded by violent, hardened criminals. It was heartbreaking. All of us at Chickie's Bail Bonds were concerned about how he would fare with his new life in state prison.

After his incarceration we maintained contact with Marcos and with his wife, receiving many letters thanking Chickie's Bail Bonds for our support and updating us on how he was doing. The letters revealed that, surprisingly, Marcos was doing quite well.

Marcos had taken it upon himself to make the most of his time in prison by teaching Bible class to the other inmates. His classes had become so popular that prisoners would follow him everywhere around the prison—like bodyguards—making sure no one could touch him. Marcos told us that he was right where he needed to be, that it was God's will that he had been put there. He felt that he had everything going for him. I was delighted by his positive outlook. His appreciation and gratitude for his new life after enduring such a terrible tragedy was remarkable.

Sooner or later tragedy happens to us all. It's how we deal with it that truly matters. There's an old adage that comes to mind: "When one door closes, another one opens."

Bob was still married when we took our first trip away together. He knew that I had never been to The Catskills, a sacrilege for a nice Jewish girl like me. Bob warned me it was no longer what it was years ago when now-famous entertainers tried out their new material to Jewish families escaping the summer heat of New York. It was still a historical experience for me.

I relished the thought of finally being able to spend our entire days and nights together, instead of him having to leave to go back home.

Walking to our hotel, we passed a jewelry store with a window display featuring an array of tiny colorful gift boxes, which I admired. Attentive as ever, Bob disappeared into the jewelry store and returned a few minutes later, carrying a bag full of the precious little boxes, each one a different color. I absolutely loved them!

"What can I use them for?" I mused aloud. Without skipping a beat, Bob cheerfully responded. "They're for you to store all of your happy memories."

Delighted by his response I reflected on how fun Bob was to be with. I wanted to somehow store this happy memory in one of those tiny colorful boxes. But how could I possibly be happy when once a day he disappeared for a short while to check in with his wife? It just killed me.

Once we got back to our hotel room, Bob lay on the bed wearing a mischievous smile and began to serenade me with his version of the Nat King Cole song, "For Sentimental Reasons."

Bob brought a tear to my eye as he sang, "I love you for

sentimental reasons," and then made me laugh when he changed the words to, "for sex-and-mental-reasons."

Bob and I dissolved into laughter. Another happy memory for the gift boxes.

That night when he slipped out of the room to make the phone call, I cried because he wasn't mine. As nearly perfect as all of it was, I could not reconcile myself being with a married man. The sad thought of ending up like my friend Charlene ate away at me. After wasting all that time on a married man, she ended up alone. The entire situation was messing with my head.

I had been seeing a therapist for many months and when she had asked what she could do for me, I told her I needed her help in making a decision. I had three options running around in my head. One, to learn to live with my situation of being with a married man. Two, to have that situation change, for Bob to divorce. And three, to have the strength to say goodbye.

After my most recent therapy visit, I made plans to take my kids to Hawaii for a week, never mentioning one word to Bob.

A few days before I was leaving, Bob and I went out to dinner just like any other night. Except that night when we had finished eating, I looked him straight in the eyes and told him, "This is the last time I'm going to see you." Then I got up from the table and walked away, without looking back.

And that was that.

Bob would call my home office incessantly, asking my secretary where I was. I had instructed her to tell him that I was fine and that everything was fine. But I wasn't fine.

I was so sick on the airplane to Hawaii I thought I was going to die. Feeling gutted emotionally and being thrown around from turbulence made for a bad combination.

In the tropical paradise of Hawaii, I was able to relax and put my mind on other things, getting involved with my kids, and enjoying the beautiful weather. A welcome reprieve. I felt a calmness and a certainty in my decision to end things with Bob.

When I returned home a week later, I was determined to get back to work and back to a sense of normalcy.

Almost immediately upon my arrival home I was greeted by my business phone ringing off the hook. Expecting it to be a potential client I answered without thinking. Of course, it was Bob.

"No. I'm not going to see you," I calmly stated, preparing to hang up the phone.

"Look, I'm getting a divorce with or without you."

There was a pregnant pause. It was the first time the word had ever been spoken. My mind was racing; my calmness and certainty went out the window. I remember thinking, *Is this what I truly want? Should I give him a chance? Will he actually follow through on this?*

He sounded so sincere that I felt inclined to believe him. He would be worth the wait. True to his word, Bob got a divorce. And we became an official item.

After the gut-wrenching tragedy I had endured in losing Fred, I thought I had lost everything. But I came to realize I was being given a second chance at love and a second chance at life. A door had closed for me and another one had opened. And I was about to walk through it.

-15-

KILLING FOR LOVE

In the bail bond business, it is essential to be an impartial participant, but I felt overwhelmingly compelled to find out what would drive my client John Johnson to murder.

The criminal justice system works best when the people involved keep their personal feelings separated from the proceedings. It's important to let the system do its work to establish guilt or innocence. I always tried to balance this aspect of the profession with empathy. It was what made Chickie's Bail Bonds different.

When my phone rang at 7:30 a.m. I had no idea I would be drawn into one of the most unusual cases I would ever experience. I was tying my aerobic shoes, getting ready for an early morning Power Pump class with my instructor Becky. Power Pump was all the rage in the '90s. It was a high intensity class filled with barbells, lunges, and an overabundance of spandex.

The answering service connected me to the caller, Alice Harper. After introducing myself she frantically asked me all the usual questions. "Can you get my father out of custody?" "What will it take?" and "How soon can we do this?"

I automatically began pulling my aerobic shoes off. Becky's Power Pump class would have to wait.

Alice and her mother, Fran Johnson, the wife of the accused, lived in Orange County, not too far from my home in Manhattan Beach. Rather than go over all of the details by phone, we agreed to meet at a Hilton Hotel, halfway between us.

I realized time was of the essence as I threw on my black slacks and jacket and a black derby hat to cover my messy morning hair.

Arriving early, I looked for the perfect table—one that was outside the earshot of other diners yet noticeable enough that my two clients would easily spot me. On the phone I had told Alice to look for the woman in the black hat.

Alice and her mother sat down with quite a tale to tell. Alice explained that her father, 79-year-old John Johnson, was being held on a one-million-dollar bond for having shot and killed her ex-husband. As Alice spoke, I could see how much her father meant to her, despite the fact that he had just killed the father of her son. Mrs. Johnson remained silent; her grief evident, dabbing a handkerchief to her red-rimmed eyes.

I delicately asked what had happened on that fateful day. Alice explained that her ex-husband Michael had visiting rights with their young son Ray. Every Sunday, Michael would come by the house where Alice lived with her parents to pick up Ray. On this particular Sunday, John Johnson had made certain his family would not be at home when Michael arrived.

When the doorbell rang, John met Michael at the front door. Without a word, John fired a shot directly at Michael, striking him in the shoulder. Covered in blood, he staggered up the street as John relentlessly pursued him and emptied the entire magazine of bullets into him as neighbors looked on in horror. Leaving Michael dead on the ground, John returned home and called the police, informing them of what he had done.

John was charged with first-degree murder—a serious homicide charge which applies to any intentional killing, willful and premeditated with malice aforethought.

Alice and her mother expressed tremendous love and support for John. They knew he would be able to build a stronger defense outside of custody and they would do anything to post his bail. We determined the family home would serve as collateral, and the wife and daughter would pay the substantial premium of $100,000.

I assured my clients their loved one would be home before nightfall. They expressed their deepest thanks and we parted ways. There was so much about the circumstances surrounding the murder that I found perplexing, but not wanting to press Alice and her mother for any more upsetting details, I proceeded to the jail to post John's bond.

There had to be more to the story. Why would this 79-year-old man, a war veteran, a devoted father and husband, murder his ex-son-in-law and leave his precious grandson to grow up without a father?

From the time I was a little girl, my fantasy was that one day my father would come home, and we would all be a happy family. Growing older, I accepted that this was one dream that could never become reality.

Oh, the fantasies I conjured up! That one day my parents would be reunited, and I would have a real family with a mother and a father. That one day my mother would not have to go to work every day to support my sister and me. That one day I would have a dad who would admire me, appreciate me, giving me a sense of who I was. His special little girl.

"Dad." The word was completely foreign to me.

My mother left my father when I was two years old. I felt sorry for my older sister, Reba, who had been ripped away from her father at the age of ten.

They say you can't miss what you've never had but that's not always true. For me there was always an emptiness, a feeling that something was missing. Not having a father meant that I was different, maybe lacking something, maybe just not good enough. All of my friends at school had fathers who took an interest in them, who loved them. I remember looking on with envy in the playground as fathers would play with their children.

Why not me?

My father visited us a few times while I was growing up. He had moved to California and lived close by. I assumed when he visited, he had come to see my sister. The beautiful "perfect" daughter in his eyes, I assumed.

On one of the rare occasions he came around, I proudly played a song for him on the piano. When I finished, he shouted, "Don't stop!" I was ecstatic. I thought he loved my playing, until he looked up at my sister's canary in the nearby birdcage and added, "The bird likes it." I was devastated. No wonder I dislike playing the piano for anyone.

When my daughter Karen was born my father came back into my life on a more regular basis. He insisted on being called Joe—not dad or grandpa.

Every Sunday morning, Joe would pick up bagels, marzipan, and cream puffs at the Fairfax Avenue Jewish Bakery and stop at our house in West Covina for a late breakfast: scrambled eggs and fried potatoes with lots of steaming hot coffee. It was then I got to know a little about my father, the man who always drove a big white truck. A farmer not just by trade—it was in his blood. He loved farming to such a degree that when asked what he'd like to do on vacation, he would always answer "farm."

My father's hands were overly large, tanned, and rough-looking with many callouses. My sweetest memories are of how he adored my children. He would grin from ear to ear as he fed my two-year old son Mitch, his giant hand clumsily trying to maneuver the tiny baby spoon into Mitch's mouth.

On the few occasions when my mother's visit happened to overlap with my father's, she would head to the backyard patio to smoke her beloved Chesterfields the moment she spotted his white truck pulling up. Sometimes the scenario was reversed; Joe would be the one to take refuge away from my mother, smoking his Lucky

Strikes on the patio.

There was one time I miraculously managed to get my mother and father seated at my dinner table. And still they refused to say one word to each other. I tried not to burst out laughing as my mother turned to me and said, "Chickie, ask Joe to pass the salt."

That was as good as it got between the two of them. For all the years they were divorced, my father refused to say one word to my mother, not even when my sister was hospitalized.

There was one Sunday I was not feeling well and lying in bed. Joe shocked me when he appeared at my bedroom door, his large, calloused hands cradling a delicate china cup. "I thought this tea would make you feel better," he said. I was flabbergasted by his thoughtful gesture. In my heart of hearts, I know my father did care for me.

I've often wondered what my life would have been like if I had grown up with a father. I know my mother had her reasons for leaving him. Part of me wishes I had been given a choice.

In most cases it is my son Mitch who meets with our newly released defendants. In the case of John Johnson, I was curious to meet him—I had many questions that only he could answer, hoping he would reveal what would prompt him to commit murder, depriving his beloved grandson of his father.

As I waited for John outside the Manhattan Beach Coffee Bean, I contemplated what kind of man could commit such a vicious murder.

I was surprised when an older, attractive, white-haired gentleman climbed off a motorcycle and walked toward me, introducing himself with a smile and an outstretched hand to shake mine. He was presentable, respectful, and pleasant. We sat, enjoying a cup of coffee as I proceeded with the usual paperwork, speaking very little about the charges he was facing. I had to be patient because I didn't want to seem as though I was interrogating him.

I kept imagining what his wife and daughter were going through, not to mention John's grandson, Ray. This poor child not only lost his father but now faced the possibility of losing his grandfather.

John revealed to me that his attorneys wanted him to plead "not guilty because of PTSD." John had been held in a prisoner of war camp for eighteen months, captured by the Japanese in World War II. PTSD has been recognized by many courts in U.S. jurisdictions.

John vehemently disagreed with their suggestion. Surprised, I asked him why he didn't want to use PTSD as his defense.

"I want the court to know the truth," he said with a look of intensity. "I want them to know why I did it."

I held my breath. *What was he about to confess? Was John truly a cold-blooded killer after all?*

"I was protecting my grandson."

At my confused look John proceeded to tell me that his former son-in-law was an alcoholic and had the bad habit of driving drunk. Distressed that his son-in-law would get into a fatal crash with his grandson while driving drunk, John took it upon himself to make sure it would never happen—by killing his son-in-law.

In John's mind his actions were justified. He had simply taken the steps he felt were necessary to prevent his grandson from being killed by a drunk driver. This was what had caused this mild-mannered man to commit murder.

I was certainly familiar with the impact of losing a loved one to a drunk driver. The pain never goes away.

At the trial of Fred's murderer, Harlene Marshall, a volunteer from MADD (Mothers Against Drunk Driving), showed up at every court hearing to support me and always bearing my favorite treat—a Hershey bar with almonds. It meant a great deal to me having her there while I had to endure listening to the testimony of Fred's murderer.

Harlene had lost her only son to a drunk driver, and also her husband who died of a broken heart in the same year. It was a double whammy. Having Harlene in the courtroom made a tremendous difference—having somebody to hold my hand while the defense attorney tried to get his client off after committing the very obvious crime of killing my husband.

Following the trial, I became an active participant in the MADD program, appearing on stage regularly as part of their Victim Impact Panel. I would speak of my tragedy along with several other speakers whose lives were also forever changed by drunk drivers. We told our stories to an audience of men and women who clearly would have rather been anywhere else; their appearance ordered by the court. They resented being in that audience, listening to our horror stories.

By the end of the evening there were tears and promises from the offenders never to repeat their bad behavior, which made the reliving of our tragedies worth it.

One story that haunted me was a young woman who had lost her only child, her precious five-year-old daughter taken for her last car ride by her alcoholic father. I couldn't help but think, *Is this what could have happened if John had not shot his son-in-law? Could this have been his story?*

I had gotten John Johnson out of custody, free to spend time with his family on my one-million-dollar bond. He was grateful for my help and relieved to be free for the moment.

One night after a MADD event, I found myself unable to sleep, tossing and turning while thinking about John's crime. I wanted to understand. Sitting down at my desk at three in the morning I penned a letter in what I felt could be John's voice about everything that had happened leading to the tragic events of that day:

I sat there waiting for the police and the dire consequences to follow. I thought back to what had brought me to today. I remembered the wedding—Alice and

Michael—the perfect couple.

Alice was striking in her white gown—brocade, she called it. Her long blonde hair made her look taller and older than her eighteen years. Sure, they were young, but so much in love and such a beautiful couple. I remember thinking at the wedding that they would have beautiful children.

Alice, my younger daughter, was always my favorite. I assume it was because her older sister Linda was born while I was overseas, and I missed all of those early months and years. When I held Alice for the first time, I promised myself that I would never let anything hurt my daughter— ever.

Alice and Michael had a good marriage. They were happy together—even more so when their son, Ray, was born. How I loved that little tyke—especially introducing him to all the "boy" things I missed with my two daughters. He loved baseball and going to the games with his "Papa."

Michael was a hard worker in a highly competitive business: car sales. No matter how hard he tried, those flashy new cars remained on the lot. More and more, he would find himself stopping at the local bar for "just a quick one" before going home and seeing Alice's expectant expression turn to disappointment.

I had no problem "helping out a bit." I told him not to mention to Alice the few dollars I "loaned" him. I still had confidence in Michael and applauded my daughter when she took a part-time job (just "temporary") to help out until Michael got back on his feet.

I vividly remember when things got really bad … the beginning of the end. Alice, Michael, and Ray were over for dinner. Ray insisted on sitting next to "Papa," much to my delight. Alice seemed a bit preoccupied, although Michael was his usual charming salesman self.

When Alice's powder-blue sweater slipped off her right shoulder, I saw the ugly bruise before she could hide it again. I didn't want to upset the dinner my wife had lovingly prepared and pretended I had not seen anything. After dinner, I told Alice I wanted to show her the blooms on my rosebush. I walked her to the backyard.

At first, she denied what had been so apparent to me. Then she finally confessed the truth: Michael was under so much pressure at work, he drank to "let off steam." On a couple of occasions, he had become abusive. She admitted his drinking had become a serious problem and that she had forbade him to drive when Ray was in the car.

I could hardly contain my anger, but Alice begged me not to say anything to Michael or anyone. She'd had serious discussions with him, and he was very sorry for what he'd done and promised to go to AA. I reluctantly agreed to keep quiet.

It must have been about ten days later when Alice called from her waitressing job at Dinah's Diner and asked me to meet her at a nearby law office, a respected firm specializing in divorce cases.

When I reached the law office fifteen minutes early for our 2:00 appointment, Alice was already in the waiting room. The heavy makeup on her face couldn't quite cover the black-and-blue marks surrounding her left eye.

I composed myself sufficiently to sit down and listen to Alice's awful story. Two days earlier, Michael had become enraged when Alice insisted he had a drinking problem and needed to go to AA. What I saw on her face was only part of the damage he had done to her before she was able to call 911 and have him arrested.

Their divorce went through. Michael begged for another chance, but Alice wisely stuck to her resolve. She was awarded full custody of Ray. Michael could not object to this with a spousal abuse charge hanging over his head. He was allowed visitation with Ray every Sunday. He was careful to never appear intoxicated during these visits.

There is no greater blow in life than losing a child. When we learned that Alice's neighbor and friend Phyllis had suffered the ultimate loss, we were all devastated. Phyllis's precious five-year-old daughter, Melony, had gone to the hardware store with her dad, Paul. As Paul approached the railroad tracks—a second beer clutched between his thighs—he could see the red lights blinking signifying an approaching train but the warning arms were not yet in place. Paul said to Melony, "Watch this, honey, here we go." They were the last words his five-year-old daughter would hear.

Melony's funeral was Saturday—just yesterday. All during the funeral I kept looking at Phyllis. She was a shell of a woman. Her clothing much too large for her shrunken frame. Her drawn face hidden behind enormous sunglasses. I could only think, *This could have been my daughter*.

It was during that sleepless night I remembered my promise to that tiny baby in my arms that I would never allow anything bad to happen to her. I had not protected her from her abusive husband, but I would never allow her to suffer as I had seen her good friend suffer yesterday.

No, my grandson would be safe from his drinking father—and I saw to it.

The lawyers wanted to use the PTSD defense, but my letter presented another possibility.

John appeared with his wife and daughter by his side at his first court appearance. Although his expression was stoic, I'm sure he was absolutely terrified of what the future might hold.

John's attorneys had convinced him that protecting his

grandson from the possibility of a drunk driving accident caused by his alcoholic father was unlikely to grant him an acquittal. Instead, they presented John's history to the jury, that he was an army veteran who continued to suffer from lingering mental distress, emotional dysregulation, flashbacks, and dissociative episodes otherwise known as PTSD.

While the defense team did an excellent job representing their defendant with this credible theory, they failed to convince a jury of his peers.

John was convicted of first-degree murder with premeditation. The death penalty was taken off the table, but John was sentenced to 25 years in prison. And at age 81, this meant he would be incarcerated for the rest of his life.

John's case continued to haunt me for the months that followed, until one day, while reading a local Orange County newspaper, my eyes fell on an article: "Convicted Murderer Dies in Custody."

I gasped.

It was John Johnson. The cause of death was listed as a case of pneumonia. An abrupt ending to an unhappy tale.

We'll never know if John's crime actually averted a different kind of tragedy or not. One thing I do know is that his grandson will grow up without ever knowing his father—wondering what's missing, feeling a little bit different from everyone else, and not knowing why.

-16-
PUSHED TO
THE EDGE

Dawn was breaking on the Channel Islands Harbor community when an ex-lifeguard awoke to cries for help coming from the nearby waterway.

Hurrying downstairs, the man ran to the end of the dock and dove into the freezing water where he discovered a woman and a young girl floating face-down unconscious along with a little boy helplessly flailing in the water.

The man was able to successfully rescue nine-year-old Sonny, his six-year-old sister, Harpreet, and their mother Narinder Virk.

The police arrived, and following their preliminary investigation, Narinder was placed under arrest, her children taken into juvenile protective custody.

I was enjoying breakfast when the call came through from Federal Prosecuting Attorney Firdaus Dordi, whom I had previously known from federal court. He described this case and how anxious he was to help. "This woman does not belong in custody."

Pushing my plate of breakfast aside, I grabbed my yellow pad and asked him for the particulars. He began by explaining that this was a personal issue for him. He had found out about Narinder's plight early on and, after spending a day in court listening to the proceedings, he knew he had to get involved.

Narinder was facing two counts of attempted murder for the incident at the harbor, charges that could keep her in prison for life, with bail set at a whopping $500,000.

She was pleading not guilty by reason of insanity, but still had many months left to wait in custody before her trial. The Deputy Public Defender Christina Briles had contended that her client was illiterate and impoverished and posed no flight risk. Briles, however, was unsuccessful in her motion before the court to have Virk's bail lowered to $50,000.

Upon hearing of Narinder's crime, I admit I was horrified. It was an unforgivable act. *Who could do that to their own children?* I thought.

That was before I learned more about what led to the crime. It was so much deeper than I could have ever imagined.

Firdaus asked me to join him at the home of Dr. Marwah to meet with a group of like-minded people about aiding Narinder. Dr Marwah, known as Los Angeles's dentist to the stars, and his wife were both Sikh and active members of the South Asian community.

Also present was Nina Sloan—a well-spoken woman in her 60s. Nina was a retired county employee who, like Narinder, was born and raised in India's Punjab province and had closely been following the case, attending all of Narinder's bail hearings.

Entering the Marwah's living room, I felt as if I had been transported into an Indian palace. I was in awe as my eyes took it all in. Colorful fabrics adorned the windows and furniture. Magnificent artwork was displayed on the walls. Everywhere I looked there were impressive brass and ivory artifacts. Even the Indian delicacies and teas that were brought out were presented on beautifully painted China plates.

There was an intense almost electrical feeling in the room, that we were about to do something very important.

After introductions were made, Nina jumped right into the matter at hand and asked me what would be required for me to post a half-million-dollar bond for Narinder. At my answer, Nina's brow furrowed with a look of concern going over the numbers in her mind.

Dr. Marwah chimed in, "What forms of collateral would be

acceptable?"

It was a question that I am often asked.

I explained to Dr. Marwah that collateral is any asset that can be turned into cash in order to pay the court's demand should a bond be forfeited. In other words, if Narinder ran away and didn't show up for court. The bail agent has six months to find a defendant; if we fail to bring the defendant back to court, we must pay the full amount of the bond. I told him real estate was the most commonly used collateral, particularly on bonds of this size.

Emotions ran high as the group wrestled with the dilemma. What could be used for collateral and how could they raise the money to cover the premium?

A daunting feat.

"We need to do something to help Narinder immediately!" Nina exclaimed with a catch in her throat. She seemed near tears as she pulled herself together.

Nina had become deeply involved with this case, visiting Norinder at the Ventura County Jail for months, going from a stranger to a supporter to a close friend. At this point, Nina knew Narinder better than anyone.

At the age of 18, Narinder had an arranged marriage to 21-year-old Santokh Virk. He wanted someone who could cook, keep house, and produce children—a role acceptable to Narinder as a young woman reared in India's village culture where female subservience was the norm.

Sponsored by her husband, Narinder came to the U.S. from a small farming village in Punjab where she had been raised in abject poverty. She had not received an education and could not read or write Punjabi or understand English.

A couple of years after their son was born, Narinder watched helplessly as her marriage morphed into a sinister game. Her husband had kept her isolated, blocking long-distance phone calls, and restricting her every movement. He owned a liquor store and started drinking. That's when the physical abuse began, screaming matches, death threats. Anything her husband could do to hurt Narinder, he would.

Santokh would leave without warning and stay away for months at a time, never letting Narinder know where he was going or when he would be back. She would be left without money or any way to support herself and with no food to feed her children.

The breaking point came when Narinder discovered that her husband had returned to India and intended to file for divorce. For Narinder, this was the ultimate shame. In much of India a divorced woman is branded for life, considered no longer pure, and thought of as inadequate for not being able to keep her man.

Too much for one person to withstand, Narinder dressed her two young children, took them by the hand, and walked them toward the darkened harbor waters.

A grievous sequence of events.

Sadly, the subjugation of wives was a reality that both the Marwahs and Nina were all too familiar with. Nina spoke of how widespread wife battery was in the South Asian community, a culture that valued complete subordination of women. Wife battery was often brushed off or never spoken of, but it existed.

Nina's voice began to tremble as she spoke, "I know what a battered woman goes through."

Revealing that she had been a victim herself and had survived two terrible marriages, Nina stated that she knew what the effects of years of physical and mental abuse could do to a person. Nina wasn't going to let Narinder suffer anymore—and I was going to do everything in my power to help.

We spent hours at the Marwah's home weighing different ideas on how to raise enough money to free Narinder. The group rallied around the idea of forming an organization devoted exclusively to helping battered women. The funds raised by this group would go toward not only helping Narinder with her situation, but other abused South Asian women as well. For too long, too many people have either denied that the problem existed or explained it away as culturally acceptable. These women's voices needed to be heard. And so, the South Asian Battered Women's Organization was formed.

We weren't just defending a woman; we were defying a culture of silence.

The first official meeting for the South Asian Battered Women's Organization happened one week later.

Dozens of women attended, each with a harrowing story to tell. I was honored to be one of the speakers addressing the group.

After explaining the concept of bail-bonds, I launched into a plea to raise funds to enable Narinder's release. "I do not dispute the severity of the crime she committed," I began, "it was a terrible thing that Narinder attempted to do. But there are extreme extenuating circumstances in her case. She felt she was without hope, without support, without solutions. What else was she to do? My main point here today is that, in our country, the accused is innocent until proven guilty. Since Narinder is considered innocent, she should not remain in custody a solitary moment longer."

My speech was met with scattered applause. Some people in the audience were convinced by my argument, whereas others regarded Narinder's act as too contemptible to look past and refused to support her. Still, I stood by what I said. Narinder deserved to be freed.

The pool of funds raised by the organization's efforts steadily grew and grew. We were having an impact! The Marwahs and Nina were quite generous, donating substantial cash resources and their homes as collateral. Nina offered to put up all her personal property—two rental houses, her bank certificates of deposit, and jewelry. I also made a donation of my own personal funds, but as much as I wanted to reduce the sizable premium of the bond, legally, I could not. The law demanded that I collect a ten percent premium or risk losing my bail license. But what I could offer them was my time, effort, and my extensive experience with the criminal justice system. I knew what Narinder was up against.

It took persistence and additional fundraising events, but at long last there was enough cash raised to pay the ten percent premium and sufficient real estate provided as collateral for the bond to be posted. Finally, Narinder was released from county jail custody to await her day in court. Her new freedom allowed her to meet with her court-appointed attorney and prepare for her defense.

Weeping and expressing gratitude, Narinder thanked her supporters in her native language, clinging to their arms as she shuffled outside the jail. Her release was bittersweet as a court order forbade her to see her children. And she was still destitute, without any prospects for finding employment.

Once again, the community rallied to help, providing financial and emotional support as well as helping her obtain work as a caretaker for a bedridden Parkinson's patient.

Narinder's future still remained uncertain, but she knew that she was not alone.

As word got out about Narinder's case, a rare unity was brought to the diverse and somewhat splintered Indian-American community. At every one of Narinder's court hearings, Sikhs, Hindus, Christians, Parsis, and Muslims packed the courtroom in a strong show of support.

Believing cultural factors were at the heart of the case, supporters rallied around her. Petitions filled with signatures circulated, all in the hope of persuading prosecutors to reduce the charges.

Many more months went by until Narinder was at last able to have her day in court. Again, the Ventura County Superior Court courtroom was full of Narinder's supporters, strangers from all walks of life, from all over the country, who had been touched by her story.

Testifying in court, Narinder wore a light-green traditional Punjabi scarf as she wiped away tears. Through an interpreter she spoke of her travails with her husband and everything that led her to that fateful decision. Her narrow shoulders hunched over, her eyes downcast. A broken woman.

After a three-week trial, Narinder was found guilty by reason of insanity. Prosecutors had argued that Narinder deliberately tried to murder her children to get back at her husband for filing for divorce. The verdict didn't come as a surprise to anyone. But the judge carefully weighed her circumstances, taking into consideration Norinder's mental health at the time she committed her crime, and sentenced her to two years at the Patton State Hospital rather than the dreaded state penitentiary.

Narinder's lenient sentence and release two years later didn't diminish the painful aftereffects of her absence. To add insult to injury, custody of her children went to her husband.

Sadly, abuse charges were never brought against Narinder's husband. Meanwhile Sartokh had found a new wife to become a mother to Narinder's children, and they all departed for India.

In the years that followed I never forgot about Narinder Virk, often wondering how she was doing. *Was she still in the hospital or had she made it out? Did she ever reunite with her children? Or did her children banish her from their lives forever?* The thoughts haunted me.

Some 15 years later I was invited to attend an afternoon party at the Marwah's home for a special reunion of all the people who had supported Narinder Virk.

Accompanied by Dr. Bob to their beautiful home, with all of those magnificent artifacts and the palatial living room as wonderful as I remembered, Dr. Marwah served a delicious lunch filled with Indian delights. Over 20 guests—mostly of Indian descent—were in attendance, each of whom had played a part in the Narinder story.

We were all overjoyed when Narinder Virk made her

appearance in an attractive Indian dress. Everyone cheered and embraced Narinder as she made her way through the crowd. Many people wept tears of happiness.

Narinder was a diminutive, slender woman, but with an inner strength that had somehow kept her going, in spite of all her hardships. Although smiling, her eyes belied the irreversible torment that would forever remain with her.

I was thrilled to have the opportunity to speak directly with Narinder. She was tentative with her English, but understandable. Narinder expressed how pleased she was to be free of the charges brought against her and thanked me profusely for my part in granting her freedom.

With some trepidation I inquired about her family life. "Have you heard from your children?" I asked.

Narinder's face lit up as she explained that her son and daughter were now full-grown adults who had warmly accepted her back into their lives. Her son lived in Sacramento, while her daughter was married and resided in India with her husband and child.

Narinder excitedly told me that her son had visited her in Los Angeles and that she was planning to travel to her old home in India, where scores of relatives were anxious to welcome her—including her daughter and grandchild. How absolutely delighted I was to hear this!

As Narinder moved on to talk to another supporter, I scanned the crowd of people who had stood by Narinder through her darkest time. Laughing, crying, embracing. In all of my years in the bail bond industry I had never seen such an outpouring of support as I did for Narinder Virk.

Narinder had been held captive for a long time: her culture, her husband, jail, and a mental hospital. For the first time in her life Narinder was truly free.

-17-
AND THE MUSIC FADES AWAY

Chickie, I need you to get to the Alhambra Police Station as quickly as you can to post a one-million-dollar bond for Phil Spector."

Whenever Robert Shapiro called it would involve an interesting case and a high-profile client. Shapiro is best known for being a member of the "Dream Team," attorneys that successfully defended O.J. Simpson against the charge that he murdered his ex-wife Nicole Brown Simpson and her friend Ron Goldman.

Over the years, Shapiro has represented many famous defendants such as the Kardashians, Darryl Strawberry, Jose Conseco, Linda Lovelace, Rod Stewart, Chaka Khan, Christian Brando, Lamar Odom, Billy Preston, and Johnny Carson.

Now he was representing Phil Spector. I wracked my brain. *Phil Spector?* The name sounded familiar, but I couldn't quite place it. My hesitation on the line was enough for him to ask, "You *do* know who he is, don't you?"

As I continued to draw a blank I simply answered, "I'll be there as soon as I can."

I quickly logged onto my computer to research Phil Spector. When the search revealed who he was, I was in awe. This was the man behind many timeless recordings and legendary artists. The Ronettes, The Crystals, Ike and Tina Turner, The Righteous Brothers, and so many others. He had also produced The Beatles' album *Let It Be*, solo albums by John Lennon and George Harrison, but most of all had made musical history with his "wall of sound" technique.

Clearly, this man was a very big deal in the music industry.

I pulled up the internet and easily found the following:

"Official reports stated that on February 3, 2003, police had gone to Spector's Los Angeles mansion after receiving an emergency 911 phone call. They found the body of the actress Lana Clarkson sitting slumped on a chair in the foyer. She had been shot in the mouth; a blue-steel .38 Colt revolver with a two-inch barrel lying near her body. The weapon was recovered and Spector was taken into custody at the scene."

No explanation was given regarding Clarkson and Spector's relationship.

It was believed that she and Spector had arrived at his house at approximately 3:30 in the morning, and less than two hours later, she was dead.

So much of the case was shrouded in mystery. *Was it a self-inflicted gunshot? If Phil did shoot Lana, what was his motive? Was it an accident or was he being framed?*

One article stated that over the years Spector had become increasingly eccentric and isolated—becoming ever more in love with his gun collection.

There was enough evidence of guilt for the judge to issue the order for a one-million-dollar bond in order for Specter to be released from custody. That's where I came in.

I changed into my classic black pantsuit, grabbed my trusty briefcase, and I was off and running.

The wide staircase outside the Alhambra Police Station was swarming with media. Eager reporters, pads and pens in hand, jostled photographers balancing cameras and microphones, all crammed as close as possible to the entrance. I would have to somehow find a way through them.

Adjusting my suit lapels, I took a deep breath and began to weave my way through the crowd. With my short stature I could barely see the entrance through the sea of media.

As the press became aware of my presence, they realized I must be part of the case. Microphones were thrust into my face while lights flashed from cameras in all directions. Rapid fire questions were shouted at me:

Do you know Phil Spector?
Did Phil Spector murder Lana?
Do you think Phil Spector is guilty?
Can you tell us anything about the case?

Part of my job was to ensure my client's privacy—certainly a challenge with Spector's fame and severity of the charge.

Waving off their flood of questions, I made my way up the steps and into the building. It was a surreal feeling. By the time I had made it inside, my head was spinning. Taking a moment to catch my breath, I approached the female deputy at the open window who seemed shell-shocked. It wasn't every day a celebrity was taken into custody at the Alhambra jail. I presented her with the necessary paperwork for the posting of my bond. She seemed intimidated at the prospect and simply shook her head "no" and did not accept it. "You need to sit and wait."

A judge agreeing to a bail of one million dollars within mere hours of arrest on a murder charge was unheard of. But I knew Robert Shapiro had a reputation for accomplishing the impossible.

As for me, I was about to post a one-million-dollar bond with no premium or collateral. The only thing I had was the word of an attorney, an attorney whom I trusted and respected. I can still remember the day we were introduced. The phone rang. It was Alvin Michaelson, a respected criminal defense attorney with whom I was privileged to work. He was calling from court and said, "Chickie,

I'm standing here with Robert Shapiro … and I would like to introduce you to him."

I almost fell off my chair. *Did he just say Robert Shapiro?!*

It had been my dream to one day work with Shapiro. I respected him greatly and there he was, waiting to talk to me on the phone. It was absolutely mind-boggling.

Shapiro was the nicest man—kind, empathetic, and so easy to work with. He knew what he wanted and he got what he wanted, because when Robert Shapiro says, "Jump," you ask, "How high?"

At the Alhambra jail, hours were slowly ticking by, until finally, the deputy agreed to accept my bond. I continued to wait for Mr. Spector's release. The media kept up their vigil on the outside front steps, feverishly waiting for Phil Spector and Robert Shapiro to walk out the building.

Stepping outside for fresh air as the police department's internal paperwork processing machinations slowly continued, I overheard the mob of news reporters complaining of being starving. Many of them had been there since very early morning. I casually commented that they could order pizza delivery and went back inside.

Less than an hour later, I could see they took my advice as I watched pizza boxes being passed overhead from person to person, everyone's hands dipping into the boxes for a slice. "You want one?" asked one of the reporters between bites. I couldn't resist and took a slice with me to enjoy in the lobby while I resumed my wait.

I had been at the jail for over five hours, when to my surprise, a deputy poked his head out from the back area and said in a loud voice, "Chickie, go home."

"I'm fine," I announced cheerily. "I'm waiting to see my client and Mr. Shapiro."

"Go home!" he repeated, this time much louder. *Okay fine.* I finally got the message. Somehow Shapiro had gotten Phil Spector out of the jail through a back exit, and I no longer needed to wait.

Making my way down the front steps, I could see the puzzled looks on the faces of the weary reporters as they craned their necks to look behind me. They presumed as long as I was there it would only be a matter of time before Phil Spector and his attorney would emerge. Sadly for them, that was not the case.

Amused by Shapiro's strategy, I accepted my newfound role as a shill. I honestly felt sorry for those exhausted members of the press as they realized that they'd been had. As for me, I could only admire Shapiro's skill in not exposing Spector to the media frenzy that would most certainly have ensued had Spector appeared.

I later learned that after the bond was posted, Spector and his attorney had been whisked out of the jail's back door. Spector had been taken to a hotel, away from prying eyes and far from the anxious media. Shapiro had cleverly used the bait and switch technique—and I was the bait.

Within several days I received a call inviting me to Robert Shapiro's office. I arrived at his prestigious headquarters, ready to collect my premium and to obtain Spector's signature on my deed of trust form—the document specifying that he agreed to use his property as collateral.

Upon entering the office, I had my first up-close encounter with Phil Spector. He was a decidedly odd-looking man, short and frail with wild gray hair that seemed to have a life of its own. With his wide eyes darting around the room and nervous fidgeting he reminded me of a lost little boy, as if he couldn't comprehend how this situation had befallen him.

Pulling the deed of trust from my briefcase, I presented it to Spector. "This enables me to have a lien on your five-million-dollar mansion."

Phil looked at me with uncertainty, then quickly at Shapiro for guidance. Shapiro gave a nod of assurance and Spector proceeded to sign the papers. When I informed Mr. Spector that there was also a premium to be paid, he seemed surprised and his eyes widened even more with a look of shock. "I didn't bring a checkbook," he stated.

Shapiro intervened, saying that I shouldn't be concerned. "The check will be in the mail." And, true to his word, the check was delivered the next day.

As the criminal proceedings began for Spector, Shapiro represented his client with his characteristic brilliance using delay tactics, a method well-known in criminal defense cases. Every caution was taken to spare Spector from the media circus his appearance would have created. Delays also provided a distinct advantage to the accused as they gave time for tempers to cool and memories to fade. Spector's first court appearance was delayed four times, almost a year.

Despite having constructed this shrewd and effective maneuver, Spector insisted that Shapiro hadn't "devoted significant time or energy to his case" or "made a court appearance in months" obviously not understanding that this deliberate move was to Spector's advantage. Shapiro was foolishly fired.

Spector then hired Leslie Abramson and Marcia Morrissey, followed by Bruce Cutler and then Bradley Brunon, before finally settling on Linda Kenney Baden. Like his music, Phil Spector continued to create noise, throwing everything at the wall when it came to legal representation.

My involvement continued for a year until my office received a phone call from Phil Spector's current attorney, Marcia Morrissey. She reported that his property would now be placed with the court and used to support his one-million-dollar bail, thereby exonerating our bond. This was an attempt to avoid the customary yearly bond renewal premium—not realizing that Chickie's Bail Bonds did not charge a renewal premium. I was happy to cooperate with the attorney, releasing my hold on the property and removing our liability.

Four years after Phil Spector's arrest his trial finally began. Although I no longer had any responsibility in the case, I continued to follow along, as did the rest of the world. There was nothing ordinary in the life of Phil Spector and the ensuing trials were no exception. His case was proving to be an ever-growing spectacle, with an ever-growing media circus.

Phil Spector's defense team painted Lana Clarkson as nothing more than a washed-up B-movie actress who was depressed about her career and had subsequently committed suicide. With Lana Clarkson's blood spatter in unlikely places, such as smeared on the staircase railing, on the back-door handle, on a man's coat in the upstairs dressing room, and on a cloth in the bathroom near the foyer, it was determined a self-inflicted gunshot would not produce this type of blood splatter.

There was never any real evidence supporting Spector's claim that Clarkson's death was an "accidental suicide" and she had "kissed the gun." She was a strikingly beautiful woman looking to continue her Hollywood career, and it seemed unlikely she would have chosen such an undignified and impulsive method of taking her life. Lana had also bought herself several pairs of shoes the day before her death, certainly not something that a person intending to commit suicide would do.

Conversely, a parade of women at the trial described how Phil Spector would turn from charmer to menace, often fueled by alcohol and medication, and they each noted his penchant for waving guns in people's faces. An accident waiting to happen.

Featuring the testimony of 77 witnesses over more than five months, the trial exemplified that Mr. Spector had notoriously been involved in at least five prior gun incidents with musicians: ex-wife Ronnie Spector, John Lennon, Leonard Cohen, Debbie Harry (the lead singer of Blondie), and The Ramones.

On the eve of the murder and into the following morning, Spector had been spotted drinking at several clubs in Los Angeles. Ms. Clarkson was working as a VIP hostess at the House of Blues where Spector later joined her. According to Spector's chauffeur, at about 3:30 a.m., he drove Ms. Clarkson and Mr. Spector to Spector's faux French chateau in Alhambra.

Just after 5:00 a.m., Spector's chauffeur, Adriano DeSouza, claimed he had heard a single gunshot. He testified he had been waiting behind the house when he heard a popping sound, after which Spector emerged holding a revolver and said, "I think I killed somebody."

After 12 days weighing the evidence in Spector's first trial, the jurors deadlocked 10-2 to convict and a mistrial was declared.

The following year Phil Spector was tried again and, of course, he had gotten himself yet another attorney. After another five-month trial, with the deliberations stretching to 32 hours over nine days, the jury found Phil Spector guilty of second-degree murder.

Despite all of his different attorneys over the years, no one could pull Phil Spector's feet from the fire. The evidence against him seemed clear to the judge and jury and the legendary producer was sentenced nineteen years to life for murder.

On January 16, 2021, Phil Spector died from complications brought on by COVID-19, fulfilling his sentence to life for the murder of Lana Clarkson.

After Phil Spector's death I found it difficult to listen to the sensational music he had produced without pondering his horrendous crime and remembering that pathetic, lost little boy I saw slumped in Robert's chair.

Many believed that Phil Spector's music would be what he would be most remembered for, but it is not. Phil Spector will go down in history for his cold-blooded murder of an innocent actress, while his music fades away into the background.

-18-

CELEBRITY GONE WILD

I had been on the phone with the creator of *Girls Gone Wild* for one minute and already my blood was boiling.

Karen and Mitch watched as my cheery disposition disappeared. I was accustomed to clients eager to get on my good side because they needed my help, but not in this case. Prospective clients were forthcoming with answers to questions about assets, friends, criminal history, and most of all, they would be very respectful. But not with Joe Francis. It was the complete opposite. He was obnoxious and demeaning. I had barely uttered the words, "Chickie's Bail Bonds..." before he abruptly cut me off.

"This is Joe Francis. Steve Levine said you'd take care of me."

There was an air of superiority about him and an attitude that I should know who he was. But I had no idea, nor did I care. In fact, had he not mentioned Steve Levine our conversation would have ended right then and there. Steve Levine was a high-profile attorney for whom I had great respect. He had referred many cases to me over the years. Not wanting to damage my relationship with him, I remained on the phone as Joe continued to bloviate.

"There are six of us and we have bail that needs to be posted in Miami. I'm prepared to pay you six percent." Joe and his entourage had been released with the understanding that bail bonds in amounts varying from $10,000 to $250,000 would be posted within ten days.

His payment "offer" of six percent was ridiculously lower than the legal premium of ten percent, so I was quite annoyed. He ranted and raved about what he was willing to do and not do in terms of paying for the bonds and offered up dubious means of collateral. I could barely get a word in edgewise.

I could feel the heat rising from my neck onto my face and my blood pressure soaring through the roof as I fought the urge to slam down the phone. As Karen ran to bring me a glass of water, I looked at her and said, "I'm going to hang up."

Joe was still bellowing about something when Karen snatched the phone from my hand. She was a good mediator and had a lot of patience.

Joe and his video crew had quite the laundry list of charges including:

-Promoting sexual performance by a child
-Use of child in sexual performance
-Procuring a person under 18 years of age for prostitution
-Sale and distribution of obscene material
-Possession of marijuana
-Possession of cocaine
-Possession of oxycodone
-Prostitution
-Contributing to the delinquency of a minor
-Endeavoring to engage in racketeering activity
-Selling/giving alcohol to a minor

The fact that many of the accusations involved minors was especially troubling to me. Before I came to my senses, remembering that every accused person is innocent until proven guilty, I said I would never post a bond for charges that included crimes against children. The girls involved with Joe Francis were teenagers, but they were still minors and had been taken advantage of.

Karen made an appointment to meet with Joe Francis at his office to arrange for posting the six bonds. After that turbulent phone call, I thought it best I sit this one out.

Every fiber of my being told me to stay away from Joe Francis. Had it not been for Attorney Steve Levine, I would never have taken him on as a client. Had I acted upon my instincts at that moment, I could have avoided a lot of aggravation in the years to follow—but as they say, hindsight is 20/20.

There is a fine balance between working with jeopardous clients and keeping our attorneys happy. Loyalty was key in this business, and it worked both ways. I took extremely good care of their clients and attorneys might casually suggest I be fully covered, meaning fully collateralized before posting a bond that they had referred.

Steve Levine was one of the attorneys who would always let me know if he felt his client might be a flight risk. Unfortunately, he read Joe Francis wrong and ultimately, I was the one to suffer.

Over the years Chickie's Bail Bonds posted bail for a wide variety of famous people, including rapper Snoop Dog, director Oliver Stone, actors Christian Slater, Billy Dee Williams, and Tom Sizemore. The charges for these celebrities ranged from a simple assault (Slater) to gun and drug possession (Snoop Dog) to spousal abuse (Williams).

Bantering with Harvey Levin of *Celebrity Justice* was always interesting. I had great respect for Harvey who was a former lawyer that had pivoted into entertainment, producing popular TV shows such as *The People's Court* and would later go on to create the iconic tabloid website and television show *TMZ*.

I would run into Harvey at the various courts around Southern California where he would interview me regarding particular celebrity cases that were ongoing. He was always quite charming, knowledgeable, and valued my opinion.

I was standing at the Los Angeles courthouse fifth floor

payphones one morning, watching lawyers rushing by to their court appearances when I heard a familiar voice ring out, "Chickie!"

Wearing a baseball cap and casual clothes, I almost didn't recognize him. At that point Harvey had already become somewhat of a celebrity and had to disguise his identity in the public arena.

Taking me gently by the arm, Harvey steered me toward a more secluded area, away from prying eyes and eavesdropping ears. "I want to ask you about Robert Blake," he said with a look of intensity.

The news had reported that Robert Blake, a well-known actor and star of TV show *Baretta*, and his wife Bonnie Lee Bakley, had recently enjoyed dinner at Vitello's Restaurant in Studio City after which she had been shot in the head. Blake claimed she'd been sitting in their vehicle while waiting for his return after he had gone back into the restaurant to retrieve his gun. He said that upon his return he found his wife dead. At the time, the entire world was morbidly captivated by the unusual case.

Harvey pointed a microphone at me as I stood there squeezed between two faded wall columns. Curious onlookers pretended not to notice the television crew only a few feet away.

"Chickie, do you think Robert Blake is innocent or guilty?"

Good-naturedly, I pretended to polish an imaginary crystal ball as a way to remind Harvey of my limited ability as a psychic. "Do you believe Blake is entitled to bail?" Harvey persisted.

I mulled it over. Thinking about that poor frightened woman, pleading for her life as a gunman—allegedly hired by Robert Blake—mercilessly ended her life, I shuddered at the thought.

"The answer is in the law," I responded confidently. "Murder-for-hire falls into the category of murder with special circumstance and bail must be denied." Harvey thanked me and rushed away to find other people to interview. That's how it was with Harvey. He was always on the move, trying to get the latest scoop about a big celebrity that had gotten caught up in some nefarious activity.

When Karen and Mitch finally returned from Joe Francis's office, they both looked exhausted. Mitch blurted out, "Mom, you're not going to believe who this guy is!"

"He's the creator of *Girls Gone Wild*," Karen chimed in. I wasn't familiar with what that was, but I could tell from the look of disdain on Karen's face that it was something sordid. I almost didn't want to know.

They told me that *Girls Gone Wild* was an adult entertainment franchise created by Joe Francis in 1997, where videos typically involved camera crews at party locations engaging young (often drunk or high) college-aged or younger females who exposed their bodies and or acted "wild"—especially during spring break. The brand had become known from their late-night infomercials. Joe Francis was the creator and occasionally appeared as the "host" of the sleazy videos.

Shocked that something like this even existed I exclaimed, "How is that even legal?" But it is not my job to determine the guilt or innocence of any client—that is up to the judge and jury. My job is to get a presumed innocent person out of jail, and most importantly, make certain they show up at every required court appearance where guilt or innocence will be determined. With Joe Francis, his depravity was already displayed for all to see in his videos.

The first thing Mitch and Karen noticed in Joe's personal office was that the entire room was the color blue—the walls, furniture—everything, including the bowl of blue M&Ms on his desk. Joe was awkwardly wearing a blue business suit and tie—like a child playing dress up.

Karen told me that the first 20 minutes spent in Joe's office was an exercise in futility. Joe appeared to be on some type of stimulant. He was jittery, talking a mile a minute, and jumping all over the place. They tried to get him to sign the paperwork while he was erratically taking phone calls, dealing with personnel, and doing anything to avoid the important business at hand.

Karen finally had to order him to sit down and pay attention. At long last Karen and Mitch left Joe Francis' office with the executed documents in hand and the check to pay the premium on the nine bonds—which we hoped would not bounce.

The required bonds were posted in a timely fashion, allowing the defendants to remain out of custody until the case was adjudicated by the court. They were eventually punished with having to pay fines for their actions—a mere slap on the wrist for such a grotesque range of charges.

Over the years, we had discovered that many celebrities had unpredictable personalities. Mitch loves to tell the story about when he was in the courtroom prepared to post bond for actor Tom Sizemore, famed for his roles in Hollywood blockbuster films such as *Saving Private Ryan* and *Black Hawk Down*.

Mr. Sizemore had been required to undergo random drug testing as a condition of probation for his conviction on charges of methamphetamine possession and battery of his ex-girlfriend, former Hollywood madam Heidi Fleiss.

However, when Tom Sizemore had most recently attempted to provide a urine sample, his parole officer deemed the temperature too low to have come from Sizemore's body and that he must have concealed a supply of clean urine on his person. The ruse was revealed when Tom was asked to remove his pants.

Listening to all of this in the courtroom, Mitch had difficulty controlling his laughter as the parole officer testified about the validity of Sizemore's urine specimen—declaring that the urine sample the actor provided wasn't his and, surprisingly, neither was the penis! Apparently, Sizemore had a penis-like device attached to his body designed to fool anyone observing the procurement of the urine sample.

According to prosecutors, Sizemore had been previously caught trying to use a similar device, sold over the internet under the brand name "The Whizzinator"—which retailed for one hundred fifty dollars—with dehydrated urine and heat packs designed to keep the sample at the proper temperature.

From that day forward, Tom Sizemore would be known in our office as the celebrity with the fake penis. It always gave us a laugh.

After dealing with Joe Francis and his crew on their Miami charges, I had hoped it would be the last we'd hear from him. Unfortunately, he resurfaced in August 2013. Steve Levine had once again referred him to Chickie's Bail Bonds. Thus, our entanglement continued.

This time Steve asked us to post a $325,000 appeal bond for Joe. An appeal bond can be posted after the court has declared a defendant guilty and imposed sentence. Joe was appealing the sentence of 30 days in custody. I just couldn't say no to Steve Levine and so, against my better judgment, we posted the $325,000 appeal bond.

It is an accepted fact of the business that writing an appeal bond is very dangerous. The defendant has already been pronounced guilty, and the appeal process is generally just a method of extending the time before beginning imprisonment. I knew that was the case with Joe Francis. He had often declared that he would not spend one night in jail—what had happened to him behind bars was not anything he would discuss or contemplate putting himself in position for again.

We did our due diligence making certain the $325,000 bond was fully collateralized. The appraisal on his property was twenty million dollars, and although there were a few liens against the property, they were insignificant enough that we were very comfortable in going ahead.

The appeals case continued at a snail's pace—as appeal cases usually do. Time after time, Joe was ordered to appear and he did not show, leaving his attorneys to conjure up all kinds of creative excuses to the court to explain their client's absence.

On May 3, 2016, Chickie's Bail Bonds received notice that the court had forfeited our $325,000 appeal bond. Joe Francis had officially become a fugitive. *I knew it.* All of my reservations about representing him had been completely justified.

Immediately, we called Zeke Unger, one of our private investigators, who was able to track Joe down in Mexico where he was living quite comfortably. He avoided capture by hiding out in a heavily guarded compound and we were unable to bring him back.

When we posted this bond, we believed we were holding sufficient collateral to cover any forfeiture, but unbeknownst to us, Joe's twenty-million-dollar mansion was encumbered with over seventy million dollars in tax liens! Since government liens against a property do not show up on title reports, our due diligence was for naught. We had been foiled!

According to newspaper stories, Joe Francis was quoted in Los Angeles saying, "I'm not trying to hide at all. I'm on my way to Florida right now to turn myself in and comply with the judge's order. I would never run from justice."

Joe clearly had no problem lying.

Joe fled the country knowing full well that it would cost Chickie's Bail Bonds $325,000.

What kind of a human being does that?

Giving the accused the benefit of the doubt sometimes proved to be quite costly.

My next step was to get attorney John Rorabaugh to file a motion with the court on behalf of Chickie's Bail Bonds to set aside our forfeiture and exonerate our $325,000 bond. Our contention was that the court had failed to forfeit the bail on the four previous occasions when Joe had failed to appear without a sufficient excuse.

According to the law, the court must forfeit a posted bond the very first time a defendant fails to appear and notify the responsible agent. Had the court acted sooner, we could possibly have thwarted Joe's exodus.

If this forfeiture remained on the books by November of that year, Chickie's Bail Bonds would be responsible for paying the court the astronomical sum of $325,000.

John Rorabaugh appeared on our behalf in the Los Angeles court, and based on his excellent arguments, the court set aside the forfeiture and exonerated our bond. Suffice it to say we were ecstatic and relieved with only having to pay $35,000 in legal expenses.

Despite this experience, I continue to believe if one is good to someone that goodness will be returned. Sadly, however, there is still evil in the world and Joe Francis personifies that. I refuse to allow that incident to define me or who I am or how I believe. I almost feel sorry for Joe Francis to have to live with himself as the evil person he is. Almost. The *Girls Gone Wild* brand was eventually sold off to get the company out of bankruptcy and to alleviate the thirty-million-dollar gambling debt that Joe had managed to rack up.

Due to Mexico's extradition rules not being enforceable for criminal offenses, Joe Francis currently walks around free in another country. In the United States he still remains a wanted felon.

-19-

WHEN FACED WITH TRUE EVIL

Although many of my clients are just people who have made terrible mistakes, every now and then I would encounter someone who was an actual psychopath.

Dealing with the family of the accused is a vital aspect of the bail industry and I prided myself on going to great lengths to be supportive during their tumultuous time. I was a shoulder to cry on, an empathetic ear to listen.

As with almost every mother I dealt with, Laura Gregson was convinced that her son was innocent of the charges of which he was accused. She lived in North Carolina, and her son Carl had not been in contact with her for years. He didn't even bother to attend his father's funeral four years prior.

When Laura finally received a phone call from her long-lost son, it wasn't because he had missed her or wanted to reunite. It was because he had gotten himself into some deep trouble. Thirty-five-year-old Carl Gregson was being held in custody at the Los Angeles County Jail on charges of burglary and attempted rape.

Carl begged his mother to immediately arrange for his bail of a million dollars, that he feared for his life after having been severely beaten up while in custody. Laura was not a wealthy woman. I encouraged her to consider what she was about to undertake, what it would mean if her son would flee and she would be obliged to pay the court a million dollars.

Laura wasn't listening to my advice as she sobbed to me over the phone, "I would never forgive myself if my son was killed in jail."

The hair on my arms stood up as she explained to me all of the circumstances surrounding her and her son. It seemed to me like there were a lot of red flags.

Based on my years of experience I asked her to consider their long estrangement and whether she should risk one million dollars—an amount that could potentially leave her destitute if Carl were to flee.

"But he's my son!"

As a mother myself, this struck a chord for me. I could not imagine refusing to help my son if he was ever in trouble. Family ties always bind. Laura was resolute and insisted on proceeding. And so began the process of obtaining Carl's release.

In order to provide the funds necessary to support the collateral and the bond premium, Laura offered up the money she had saved for her retirement as well as real estate holdings. Within two days Carl was freed from custody.

Our company policy is to meet with a client once released to take their photograph, take note of their history and contacts, and explain their responsibility to stay in touch with our office, their defense attorney, and most importantly, to show up in court for each appearance. In this case, Mitch had arranged to meet Carl at a coffee shop convenient for both of them. I was in the office when Mitch called and said, "I just can't deal with this client."

I was so surprised. This was out of character for Mitch. Working closely with me throughout our years in business, I could not recall one instance where he refused to work with a client. I understood Mitch's aggravation as soon as he put me on the phone with Carl.

Carl wildly accused me of cheating his mother out of money—that our fee was exorbitant. He then dramatically ranted that we had no idea how to conduct our business. "You're doing everything wrong!" He sounded out of control, like he had lost his mind. There was no point trying to rationalize with someone who was irrational. I simply said, "Give the phone back to my son."

Mitch managed to eventually get Carl through all of the necessary steps that we require of our clients, but it was quite a feat.

Surprisingly, I received an email about a week later from Carl. He apologized for his recent behavior, saying he was completely out of line. He also stated that he felt we had treated his mother with consideration, he was grateful for our help and that, yes, we did know how to run our business. It was hard to believe that this was written by the same irrational person who had given us such a terrible time just days before. One minute I was the devil incarnate and within a few days I had become the embodiment of perfection. I knew that Carl was trouble.

Traditionally, we did not allow clients to travel beyond the state of California, especially with a bond of this size. The risk if the defendant didn't return was too great.

However, when Laura called to tell me that she was trying to arrange for Carl to fly home to North Carolina for a family reunion, I could almost feel her desperation. She sounded so hopeful about being able to see her son for the first time in years. I explained to her that if Carl skipped out, she would be liable for the bond. But her desire to reunite with Carl overcame any thought of possible risk or danger and off Carl went to North Carolina.

I was happy to hear that Carl had returned to Los Angeles within the allotted time and appeared for his court date as instructed. All seemed to be going well.

A couple of months later, Laura called me again and said that Carl wanted to return to North Carolina to see her, and she had agreed. Once again, I advised her of the risk she was taking, but she was adamant and we had no choice but to give permission. However, we made sure to hold onto Carl's passport to be certain he couldn't leave the country. This time the visit did not go as planned.

Within a week Laura called me in a panic. Carl was on the run.

Laura told me that everything had been fine for the first couple of days but then she began to notice some odd behavior, similar to what I had observed in my brief dealings with Carl. He had unpredictable mood swings and started complaining to her about his finances, and how as a family, they never had money. He even said, "You know, at that time I considered killing you and my father."

Realizing that her son was clearly unstable, Laura became very much afraid. Then Carl continued his ranting and demanded that she give him $100,000 so that he could start a new life. "I was afraid to say no," she tearfully told me.

Ultimately, he happily pocketed a check from Laura in the amount of $75,000—all she had available.

When Carl didn't appear at breakfast the next morning, Laura went to his room and found it completely devoid of his belongings. Spotting a white envelope conspicuously propped up on the dresser, Laura's hands shook as she opened it.

It was a note from Carl saying that with all the cards stacked against him, he had no choice but to leave town. And just like that, her son had become a fugitive.

There was no real explanation for what he was doing and no apology for the hurt and financial loss his act would cause. He had simply vanished.

Chickie's Bail Bonds was now facing the obligation of paying the court one million dollars—a terrible prospect—one that would ultimately have to be paid by Carl's mother.

There was no time to lose. "We have to hire a private investigator to bring your son back." Knowing she was responsible for the bail, Laura was cooperative and agreed to work with whomever we hired. The FBI also became involved in attempting to apprehend Carl on charges of unlawful flight to avoid prosecution.

Private investigator Zeke Unger came on board, diligently working with Los Angeles and federal authorities. Everyone wanted to put Carl back in custody—especially when there was strong evidence tying him to several other unsolved rape cases in Los Angeles. I was sure it was only a matter of time before he would be apprehended. At least I hoped.

Less than a week later, Laura called again, distraught. Her long-time live-in companion Roger Young had discovered that his handgun was missing. Clearly Carl had stolen it, managing to get himself into even deeper trouble, going from "fugitive" to "armed fugitive."

I felt terrible for Laura who had tried to do the best she could for her son and now was suffering. It was clear to me that no matter which way the story went with Carl, there would be no happy ending.

Those first few weeks I spoke with Laura almost every day, although it would be more accurate to say Laura talked to me. I was glad to be there for her, although it pained me to hear Laura beat herself up verbally each day. She hadn't done anything wrong. What mother wouldn't trust her own son?

"Chickie, how could I have been so stupid? Why didn't I listen to you? When Carl refused to wear an ankle monitor, I should've realized he was planning to take off."

My heart went out to her. Carl had preyed on his mother's vulnerability, her unconditional love. Why would she ever suspect that her son would take advantage of that? Why would anyone? The truth is that nobody wants to consider the horrific thought that their precious offspring might actually be a psychopath.

Making matters worse, she had rented a vehicle for him during his visit. Not only had she provided the money Carl needed to support himself as he ran from the authorities, but she had provided him with a getaway car. Laura revealed to me that she felt guilty about her inadvertent role in Carl's escape from justice.

As time went by, Laura began to spiral further down into depression, to the point where she stopped eating and became dependent on medication to catch even just a wink of sleep. She was a real mess.

It wasn't until a month later that we had our first sighting of Carl. Law enforcement across the country had been given the information about the rental car he was driving, and the vehicle was spotted in Alabama. Local police immediately gave chase, and a high-speed pursuit ensued that went on for over an hour.

Consistent with his unhinged behavior, Carl recklessly drove his car the wrong way down a one-way street. The police, not wanting to endanger innocent lives, called off the chase which allowed Carl to escape.

Within hours of the chase the local police department received a visit from a hysterical young woman who had had a terrifying encounter with Carl. Amy Collins, a young wife and mother, had just finished shopping at the local supermarket, loaded her groceries, grabbed her keys from her purse, and got behind the wheel of her black SUV. As she turned on her motor, a man appeared banging a gun on her window. He yelled for her to get out of the vehicle. Terrified, Amy hit the gas pedal and sped out of the parking lot away from the would-be assailant. After she described the perpetrator to the police, they knew that her description matched Carl's.

In the extensive search for Carl's whereabouts, every known method of apprehending a fugitive was employed both by Zeke and by federal law enforcement. Although Carl's computer, phone, credit cards, and bank account were all being closely monitored, strangely, there was no activity.

Carl did not cash the $75,000 check so it was unclear how he was able to keep himself hidden and stay alive with no money. There were no reports of any armed robberies with perpetrators matching his description.

As the months progressed, Laura and I spoke less and less. There wasn't much that either of us could do or say with the case in the hands of our investigator and law enforcement. One day she called me in a panic as she realized that an entire sheet of checks was missing from her checkbook. Laura, as many women of her generation, had relied on her late husband to handle their finances. Since his death many of her personal banking records had not been reviewed in years. *A-ha!* I thought. *So that was how Carl had managed to stay under the radar all of these months!*

Calling her bank, Laura learned that significant funds had recently been taken out of her account. She was devastated to find out that, once again, she had been swindled. Carl had the $75,000 check Laura had reluctantly given him and with all those additional checks he could enter any amount and easily forge her signature simply by copying it from her original check. Deviously cunning.

As we neared the 180-day deadline, Laura revealed to me that she believed Carl would remain in hiding and would not allow himself to be found until after she had been forced to pay the one million dollars. She fully expected that once her funds were gone, Carl would call her, absolutely gleeful that he had been successful in seeing her suffer such a terrible loss.

I found myself speechless. *What can you say when faced with true evil?*

With the deadline looming, I suggested one option for Laura to take. Although California courts demand payment of a forfeiture within the prescribed six-month period, that date can be extended with a qualified bail attorney presenting evidence to the court showing that every effort had been made to locate the fugitive, and that if the time were extended, there was a good chance he would be apprehended.

Laura heeded my advice. Attorney John Rudabaugh had an excellent reputation for pulling bail bond agents' feet out of the fire and was the obvious choice to handle this situation for us. My staff and I—plus Laura in her North Carolina home—waited for the phone to ring on the day of the hearing. If John did not succeed in persuading the court to grant the extension, Laura would be faced with giving up most of her worldly possessions to the court forthwith. It was a nail-biter.

Just shortly after twelve noon on the hearing date, John telephoned and exuberantly delivered the good news that we had been granted the additional 180 days to find Carl! The hunt continued.

For several months, there hadn't been any new sightings of our elusive fugitive. Carl had the dubious achievement of becoming number ten on the FBI's Ten Most Wanted list. They were even offering a reward of up to $100,000 for any information leading directly to his arrest, and billboards with photos of Carl's face were on major highways in several cities.

Early in the afternoon on a peaceful Saturday, Carl came out from hiding briefly when he returned to his mother's house in North Carolina. Laura's romantic partner Roger Young answered the front door. I'm not sure who he was expecting to see, but certainly he never thought it would be Carl!

Stepping outside, Roger slammed the door behind himself to prevent Carl from entering the house and demanded to know what he was doing there. Carl said he was looking for his mother, that he had come to say goodbye. Roger told Carl that his mother wasn't there, then lashed out with a tirade berating Carl for showing so little regard for his mother and putting her through such awful hell. Carl stood there emotionless, as if Roger had simply been reciting the weather report. With no further conversation or apologies, Carl turned around and headed back to his vehicle with one request, "Don't call the police."

Roger immediately ran into the house to call the police. By the time Laura returned home there were three officers wearing bulletproof vests camped out in her living room.

They informed her that they would be spending the night in case Carl made a return visit and advised Laura that if she heard any noises in the middle of the night, she should stay in her bedroom. Laura was overwhelmed by the concept that her life was in danger, targeted by the child she had brought into the world.

Carl never returned.

We were so certain that with all of our efforts to return Carl to custody, he would be apprehended during the six-month extension the court had provided. But that second window of opportunity closed, and Laura officially owed the court one million dollars.

Attorney John Rurabaugh said he felt there were sufficient facts in our favor and wanted to file another motion with the court. With nothing to lose and possibly everything to gain, Laura agreed. He filed a motion in Los Angeles Superior Court asking that the bail forfeiture be set aside and to exonerate Carl's bond that Chickie's Bail Bonds had posted.

It was only five days later I received a phone call that left me frozen in shock. Carl had been located in a small North Carolina motel earlier that morning. The FBI had burst into his room, guns drawn. He had been caught and there was nothing he could do. Carl pulled out his handgun and was immediately shot dead by the officers. Carl had maintained he would never be taken into custody and he made certain of it. Suicide by cop. A violent end to a violent man.

Laura had lost her son, and unfortunately, she was still financially obligated to the Los Angeles Court. The fact that Carl was dead didn't change anything—the payment to the court was due, however, the motion John Rudabaugh had filed was still pending.

With her heart breaking, just six weeks after the loss of her son, Laura was forced to sit in the courtroom and watch as her attorney attempted to explain to the court why she should not have to pay the outstanding one million dollars.

I had hoped the court would take into consideration the death of her son plus the great effort that had been exerted in attempting to return him to custody, but that was not to be. The judge upheld the judgment, and the full amount of the bail had to be paid.

Laura, who had only wanted to do the right thing from the very start, had to be the one to pay.

Laura lost her son and one million dollars, but the pain and emotional betrayal would remain with her forever.

-20-

TWELVE HOURS
WITH MY HUSBAND

There are rules in every line of business, and the bail bond business certainly has its share. By the same token, some rules are destined to be broken—whether one likes it or not.

When Attorney John Yzurdiaga contacted me on a Friday afternoon, I could tell by the tenor of his voice that I was about to become involved in a serious situation. And yes, a few rules were going to have to be broken along the way. I had known John professionally for many years and trusted him implicitly.

John informed me that Mr. Herman, a 79-year-old gentleman of significant means and not in the best of health, had just been taken into custody at the Beverly Hills Jail on a charge of child molestation. Because this jail lacked the medical capability to handle the elderly man's declining physical condition, the officers were preparing to whisk him to the Los Angeles County Jail, a terrible, harsh place even for the most hardened criminals. John asked me to make an exception and not require the requisite premium and collateral prior to obtaining his client's release. He stressed that we had to, "Get him out of there—*now.*"

You have no doubt deduced that this is where the "breaking the rules" part came in. I had a catch-22 on my hands. I had every faith in John's word and understood the dire circumstances involved. Mr. Herman might have been elderly and frail, but he was also being charged as a child molester. How could I possibly rationalize breaking the rules for someone who might be guilty of something so sleazy and just plain awful? How could I help facilitate putting someone like this back on the streets?

The words "might be guilty" stuck with me. Once again, I came to the same conclusion I always did: Everyone is presumed innocent until proven guilty. If I were willing to break the rules for some other client of John's, why wouldn't I do so for Mr. Herman?

Before I had a chance to explore my feelings any further, I received a call from the accused's family attorney. He pleaded with me to appreciate the urgency of the situation and assured me that he would be personally responsible for seeing to it that I received everything I needed the following day. I caved, agreeing on the spot to break my own rules.

In the meantime, precious seconds ticked away. I knew I didn't have a prayer of making it on time to the jail before my client would be transferred. I made arrangements with a bail-bond agent in close proximity of the Beverly Hills Jail to race over there and get Mr. Herman released before the transfer could take place. I subsequently called the jailor and assured him that bail would be posted forthwith, and my client should not be transferred. The jailor said he would hold off as long as he could.

Within an hour, Mr. Herman heard the clang of the heavy bars behind him as he was released on bail. He fell into the loving arms of Gracie, his tearful wife. A limousine awaited the Hermans to drive them, their best friend, and their family attorney, to their Beverly Hills home.

The more I thought about it, the more I realized I had made the right decision. I don't believe that a presumed innocent person should sit in a cell until (and unless) proven guilty in court. My job is to see that the accused does not unnecessarily remain in custody and that he or she appears in court to face the charges. If proven innocent in court, the defendant has spent as little time locked up as possible, thanks to my efforts. This is how I had always done business and it was what motivated me from day one.

What happened next haunts me to this very day. After the ordeal of Mr. Herman's arrest and release on bail, the Hermans, joined by their good friend, and the family attorney, arrived at the Beverly Hills home. At first, everyone expressed relief that Mr. Herman was safe and comfortable in his own living room with people who cared about him. They made small talk when, out of the blue, Mr. Herman announced that he intended to take his life. No compelling, impassioned argument made by his wife or friends seemed to sway his decision. The charges being leveled against him weighed so heavily that he didn't think he could "face another day."

At four in the morning after many hours of discussion, the exhausted group disbanded for some much-needed sleep. However, one specific person did not enter his bedroom. Instead of joining his wife, Mr. Herman proceeded to the garage where he retrieved a hidden pistol and shot himself in the head.

All of this had occurred within a mere twelve hours of Mr. Herman's release from custody. I grieved for him and his wife and no longer felt I deserved or wanted the premium for having posted the bond. The fact that Mr. Herman's family was wealthy was insignificant to me. How could I justify being paid after such a such a terrible event? Not to mention the fact that he had only been out on bail for a mere twelve hours.

Although I had made my decision on the matter, I contacted a senior attorney at my insurance company to be certain I was on steady ground. He informed me, in no uncertain terms, that it was absolutely necessary for a premium to be paid when a bond is issued and the accused released—regardless of any subsequent circumstances. He explained it this way: If the client had fled during those elapsed twelve hours, I would have been obligated to pay the court the full amount of the bail. Mr. Herman's suicide had no bearing when it came to interpreting bail bond premiums. My counterarguments failed to convince the attorney. The law is the law.

Well, as you know by now, this Chickie never gives up without a fight. I called the Department of Insurance—the governing body that regulates bail bonds—who gave me the same exact response. I was legally bound to collect the premium owed.

I spoke to the family attorney later that day and explained to him what I had been told by my insurance company attorney and the representative from the Department of Insurance. I said that I had to comply with the law, even though I disagreed with it. He accepted my explanation without question but requested that I wait until after the funeral to collect the premium.

A few days passed when I received a call from the attorney. He instructed me to go to the Bank of America in Beverly Hills to pick up my cashier's check.

How I dreaded the moment of that exchange! It would be an understatement to say I felt "uncomfortable" sitting in the bank waiting for a check I didn't want. I was surprised when I was called forward—not to claim the money, but to receive a phone call. I went to the branch manager's office and picked up the receiver. "Hello, this is Chickie Leventhal, how may I…"

"Chickie, this is Mrs. Herman," interrupted the shaky voice on the other end of the line. *Why is she calling me?* I wondered. Was she about to refuse to make the payment? Was she going to holler at me?

"I am so sorry for your loss, Mrs. Herman," I consoled her. "How can I help you?"

"Chickie," she paused, carefully choosing her words, "I wish to personally thank you for giving me the last twelve hours with my husband."

I was speechless. This poor woman was undergoing such emotional trauma, yet felt the need to call me at that moment to thank me? The Yiddish word *mensch* (meaning, a person of honor) is gender neutral but most often tends to be used in reference to men. Well, in this case, *mensch* certainly applied to Mrs. Herman, putting her own emotions aside and expressing her appreciation for me.

After we said our goodbyes on the phone, the branch manager handed me an envelope with a cashier's check for the full amount of the premium on a one-million-dollar bond—one hundred thousand dollars. As I looked at the check and considered Mrs. Herman's words, I reflected that perhaps this payment had served a purpose after all. Not only had I enabled the Hermans to spend their final twelve hours together and saved them the embarrassment of his trial, I had given the widow at least some closure on the matter and the ability to give back to someone who had treated them with respect and dignity.

The terribly sad case of the elderly gentleman, Mr. Herman, made me realize how short and unpredictable life could be. I thought about my life with Bob and what I could do to make it better for him.

That year for Chanukah I presented him with a snow globe, the kind children love, a snowman or Santa surrounded by swirling snow. The one I chose for him, however, was the skyline of New York. He opened his present with an inquisitive look and turned to me. I grinned from ear to ear as I said, "For Chanukah, I am giving you New York."

Bob had four grandchildren living on Long Island. I thought it unfortunate that he had these wonderful grandchildren, but living in Los Angeles he was deprived of seeing them grow up. I knew how important they were to him and decided to do something about it.

Within six weeks, we were flying to New York to meet with the realtor I had been talking with. He assured me he would show us condos for sale in Long Beach just a half hour from Bob's family and, as I insisted, with a water view. He didn't mention that February was possibly the worst month of the year to be traipsing around a beach community.

I was raised in California where the weather is always perfect. I was shocked by the temperature and the whirling wind in Long Beach. No matter how many scarves Bob wound around my head and neck, and although I was wearing the ugliest bubble coat, I was still freezing.

Jacob, a very a pleasant gentleman, listened intently when I described again exactly what we wanted—especially that view. Each of the units he showed us had a view all right—providing you stood on your right foot and squinted out a small window. I finally said, "Stop, we are done. If this is the best you can do, forget it."

A smile came over Jacob's face. "Well," he said, "there is another unit with a great view I know you'll like, but there's one drawback." I asked what that was and he told us that the condo was already sold. I couldn't help getting more than a little bent out of shape, asking why he even mentioned it. A big grin came over Jacob's face when he said, "They haven't signed yet…"

Unbeknownst to us, property in the state of New York changes ownership in a lawyer's office and not before. The fact that an offer was made and accepted between buyer and seller was not a legal transaction. Hesitantly, we agreed to see the property.

Jacob drove us down a pleasant street one block from the ocean. We entered the small lobby of a building in decent shape for its age, taking the elevator to the ninth floor. When Jacob unlocked the door and the ocean fairly hit me in the face, I said without even walking in the door, "We'll take it," and we headed for the lawyer's office where I paid full price, certain the original buyer would not have done so.

Bob and I spent as much time as we could on the East Coast, enjoying our tiny condo. The small balcony was just the right size for an evening glass of wine while watching the boardwalk parade below us and the magnificent ocean beyond. On weekends, Bob's family would come to lie around the pool while Bob enjoyed splashing around in the water with his grandkids.

The condo consisted of a minute kitchen, a small living room, a bedroom with an attached bathroom, plus a tiny powder room. The unit had seen better days, and since I loved decorating, I hired a locally advertised contractor. After a couple months of waiting for the work to start, we learned that this thief had absconded with my $25,000 deposit as well as leaving several other unsuspecting clients in the lurch. I worked with local authorities and were thrilled to hear that our scheming friend who had fled to his home country had been picked up by Interpol. Fortunately, the $25,000 had been paid on my American Express Card and I was reimbursed. The next contractor was honest and our condo was delightful!

We made good friends with our neighbors, Nancy and Silvio Berkovichi, and shared many dinners, both sushi and Italian. And Nancy and I loved our shopping escapades, leaving Bob and Silvio to enjoy each other's company.

Frequently, Bob and I would take the train into Manhattan, trains being an entirely new experience to a California girl. It was just a short trip into the magic of the city of Manhattan. This was a new world and Bob loved showing me all the wonder of it. He introduced me to the museums he fondly remembered from growing up, although he didn't share my love for the museum shops. I would bring home my memories, just as I had years before, to store in the precious little boxes Bob bought me on our early trip to the Catskills.

Being in New York gave Bob the opportunity to visit with his nieces and nephews. He had been a second father when illness took their beloved fathers, his two brothers, a terrible loss for him, as well.

It also gave me a chance to spend time with my favorite cousin, Evelyn. She introduced us to her favorite little French café where we ate early in order to attend a Broadway show. She taught me to love Broadway all those years ago. I love it even more today.

When Bob told me he wanted to take me to see the Christmas show with the Rockets at Radio City Music Hall, I was more than a little surprised. Bob and I are both Jewish and he was actually a practicing Jew. Wherever we were in Los Angeles or New York he always found a Temple to go to for Saturday morning services. My religious upbringing consisted of hanging around the steps of the Breed Street Shule in Boyle Heights where I grew up, with my girlfriends, never actually crossing the threshold.

But Bob was so adamant this show was not to be missed that my daughter Karen and son-in-law Nico asked if they could join us, and we arranged to meet them waiting in line outside the theatre. We arrived early and decided to kill some time at the Brooks Brothers store on a nearby corner where they were advertising a sale.

Bob went off to the men's department. After determining that there was nothing of interest to me in the ladies' area, I proceeded to sit down on their only chair. My "schlepping" bag, a sparkling gold shopping bag from Harrods, sat next to me on the floor. After a few moments Bob reappeared, announcing that there was nothing of interest to him. I picked up my bag and we left.

As we were still early for our rendezvous with Karen and Nico, we proceeded across the street to a restaurant where we were escorted to a table. I left Bob at the table and proceeded to the ladies' room, cell phone and gold bag in hand.

Immediately after opening my bag, I couldn't help but shout, "Oh my God, this is not my bag!" My shock came when I saw that sitting on top of my own belongings were two nicely folded beautiful silk scarves, bearing the Brooks Brothers tags, and a price of $168 each. At this point I was starting to question my sanity. How in the world did these two scarves just happen to be in my bag? Of course, as my "schlepping" bag, it was complete with all of my things.

I walked out of the ladies' room in a state of shock and confronted Bob.

"Did you put anything in my bag?"

"Of course not."

I proceeded to show him the scarves. He was as mystified as I. There did not seem to be any explanation for this phenomenon.

Bob and I left the restaurant and proceeded back to the theater where we found Karen and Nico and shared this occurrence with them. They, too, could come up with no explanation for how two brand-new Brook Brothers scarves, complete with price tags attached, ended up neatly folded in my bag.

After the performance, the four of us marched into Brooks Brothers and I asked to see the manager. When he appeared, I related the story him, explaining that I would like for him to help us solve this mystery. I presented the scarves which he took, and then proceeded to his computer.

Within a few minutes, the manager reappeared, asking if we had been to any other Brooks Brothers store that day. I responded in the negative, explaining that we had been on our way to the theater just around the corner and only stopped in this Brooks Brothers for a few moments.

At this point, the manager declared, "These are not our scarves. These scarves are part of the new fall line which we have on order. However, they have not yet been received." I repeated what he had said, saying "So, these are not your scarves, correct? So, if they are not yours, obviously they must be mine. May I have a bag, please?" The Manager graciously handed me a very nice Brooks Brothers bag into which I placed "my" scarves, and the four of us left the store.

My daughter insisted that if she had not seen this entire scenario with her own eyes, she would not believe it. The questions remained. How in the world did these scarves get into my bag? How could they not be the merchandise of the only Brooks Brothers store we went to that day? Was that guy really the manager or just a complete nutcase?

This continues to be a mystery, one recounted to many, none of whom has been able to present any explanation.

Several days later, I was on the telephone with my dear friend Flo, relating this story and when she was finally able to stop laughing, said to me, "Well, wasn't that nice, you went back to the store, showing your daughter how honesty is always the best policy and setting such a fine example for her." Sheepishly, I had to let her down when I explained in no uncertain terms that it was questionable whether I would have indeed gone back to Brook Brothers had my daughter not been with me. It is Karen who is the most upstanding, honest person in my family or anyone else's, and I knew there was no way I could walk away with those scarves in her presence. Setting an example, indeed! Flo and I laughed together.

-21-
TWO FOR THE MONEY

When Nour Tillo decided to skip town, I was faced with two choices: Take the easy way out by foreclosing on the properties of Nour's partners and use the cash collateral provided by his father, or I could hunt Nour Tillo down and bring him back to court. I chose the latter.

Tillo was co-owner of a chain of four Los Angeles health food restaurants. He had been charged and found guilty of raping one of his restaurant employees. Prosecutors said the victim was raped in Tillo's Venice apartment where they had gone to retrieve car keys she had left there before a business meeting at one of the restaurants. She was treated for bruises the next day at a hospital and the incident was reported to the police. Tillo's attorney, Mark Gottesman, argued that Tillo and the victim had consensual sex.

When Tillo was first arrested, Mark asked me to obtain the defendant's release from the Los Angeles County Jail. After meeting with Tillo's two business partners, both pleasant Middle Eastern gentlemen, I agreed to post Tillo's $150,000 bond with the partners' homes placed as collateral. During the trial, Tillo appeared as required at every court appearance—the last one resulting in his conviction.

Following the verdict, Mark Gottesman called me. I already knew what he was going to ask. "What would it take for you to post a $350,000 appeal bond for Nour Tillo?"

Mark and I had an exceptional working relationship and I

wanted to help, but I knew that with Tillo already being convicted, it greatly increased the likelihood of him taking off. I agreed to post the appeal bond, but I made certain that his business partners were willing to be responsible for the appeal bond as well as his father who provided cash collateral.

Sure enough, Nour Tillo failed to show up for his sentencing.

Technically speaking, Tillo was a fugitive and law enforcement would be responsible for tracking him down. I could have just stepped aside and foreclosed on the properties and assets. This would have placed an extreme economic hardship on the innocent indemnitors—his business partners and on Tillo's father. It would also potentially allow a convicted rapist to go free.

As I saw it, my only option was to find Tillo and present him to the court. But I was going to need some help.

Bounty hunters have the power to cross state lines to bring a defendant back to court. Without bounty hunters, most bail jumpers would never come to trial. Courts long ago decided that a defendant, in accepting a bond, is agreeing to allow the bondsman to go after him if he fails to come to court.

Bounty hunter fees are not regulated, meaning they can charge whatever they feel their services merit. It's usually between ten and twenty percent of the face value of the bail bond. Believe me, when the going gets tough, bounty hunters are worth every red cent!

For this case I chose to bring on Mackenzie Green. She was considered the best in the business, and as such, she charged the most: 20 percent of the face value of the bond, in this case $350,000.

Mackenzie was a middle-aged, five-foot tall gay woman made of solid muscle. A real powerhouse. One of the most respected bounty hunters in the business, Mackenzie always managed to locate my skips. She absolutely loved the thrill of the chase.

Mackenzie and I had a lot in common and respected each other. We were around the same age and had both started our careers in criminal justice later in life. She had been an airline stewardess and worked in real estate before becoming a bounty hunter. Like me, she knew the challenges of working in a male-dominated industry, gaining the respect of her colleagues through sheer grit and determination.

After I filled her in on the unique background of the case, she was off and running. We both were determined to bring Nour Tillo down, and I felt certain that with Mackenzie's skills, we would have our man in no time.

A few years earlier Mackenzie helped me track down a very unusual case where the defendant had faked his own death.

A highly respected attorney, Paul Takajian asked Chickie's Bail Bonds to post a $50,000 bail bond for his client Amir Saroush—an American citizen of Persian descent accused of blackmail. It was all fairly straightforward. Or so I thought.

However, on the day of his required court appearance, Amir's wife surprisingly showed up to court dressed head-to-toe in black and tearfully presented hospital records and a death certificate generated from somewhere in Iran. She informed the court that while visiting his ailing father in Iran, Amir had also fallen ill and died.

Thinking that the case would be closed and the bond exonerated, we were surprised when the prosecutor stood up and addressed the judge with what seemed like a strange request. "Your Honor, the People would like to request that the court defer the exoneration at this time."

Everyone in the courtroom gasped in unison, including me. *Why would they defer the exoneration? Why not exonerate the bond for a dead man right then and there?* If they did not, I would still be liable for the $50,000.

Even the judge seemed confused by this, asking for an explanation.

"The documents presented today are new to the People, Your Honor, and are written in a foreign language. All we ask is that we are granted some time to review and validate them."

Agreeing with their concerns, the judge decided to recommence at a later date. At the time the prosecution's review and validation struck me as just a proper formality and I wasn't the least bit concerned. I was certain the bond would be exonerated at the next court date, and that would be that.

When the court recommenced a few months later the prosecutor dropped a bombshell.

"The People have conducted a thorough review and subsequent investigation into the death certificate of Amir Saroush, and we have determined that all of the paperwork has been falsified."

We were frozen in disbelief. *The death certificate was fake?!*

The prosecutor continued, "We have every reason to believe that Amir Saroush is, in fact, very much alive. We assert that his wife, Reyhan Saroush—who had appeared before this court—lied and was in collusion with Mr. Saroush with the sole intent of defrauding the court."

Defense Attorney Paul Takajian was as shocked as everyone by this news, obviously feeling betrayed by his client. Clearly, nothing like this had ever happened to him. He profusely apologized to the court and to me. While I readily accepted his apology, I gently reminded him that he was in no way at fault. Amir Saroush had pulled a fast one on all of us.

But if Amir was alive, where was he?

The realization hit me. Suddenly I was on the hook for the $50,000 that would be coming out of my own pocket if I couldn't track down my undead defendant.

It was time to bring in Mackenzie to tackle the assignment. With all of the particulars of the case, she went right to work.

The first thing Mackenzie had to determine was whether or not Amir was in Iran. He had, in fact, gone there to visit his father, but that didn't necessarily mean that he was still there. Using her vast sleuthing skills, Mackenzie was able to deduce that Amir had left Iran.

As a United States citizen, Amir had an enormous number of countries that would take him in without asking any questions.

Mackenzie dug even deeper in her search and was able to rule out everywhere else in the Middle East. Ultimately, she tracked him down at a hotel in Cuba where he had actually registered under his own name! Not exactly the smartest thing to do for someone who was pretending to be dead.

Still, Amir had done enough homework to know that Cuba did not have an extradition treaty with the United States and therefore it was a safe haven for him from the U.S. authorities. He was perfectly happy to chat with Mackenzie on the phone, well aware there was nothing she could do to bring him to justice.

I had no other option except to claim the collateral from the indemnitor for Amir's bond who was none too pleased when I requested the $50,000 payment.

Amir had gotten away with blackmail, faking his death, jumping bail, and leaving his friend to foot the bill.

It didn't take long for Mackenzie to uncover new information about Nour Tillo. He had planned his escape from justice very carefully, buying a car under a false name and had even obtained a fake driver's license.

She also discovered that Tillo had responded to a classified ad in a newspaper looking for an experienced restaurateur who would be willing to relocate to Seattle.

I couldn't help but shake my head in awe. *How could she have possibly known that Nour would suddenly apply for a job in Seattle?*

Bounty hunters have their trade secrets for how they pursue their targets. I have no idea how she was able to find him, like trying to find a needle in a haystack. But that was how Mackenzie operated—by her intuition. A gut feeling.

Mackenzie contacted the unsuspecting business owner, and in no time, she was on her way to Seattle. Using her powers of persuasion, Mackenzie managed to convince the restaurant owner to provide her with Tillo's Seattle address.

Within a few hours Mackenzie was at the location, flanked by one of her friends—a burly off-duty cop. Although Mackenzie was tough, she never approached a bail-jumper alone, and she always made sure to alert the local authorities as to what she was doing. She wasn't a vigilante; she was a professional.

While waiting outside Tillo's house for the police to arrive before they made their move, Nour Tillo suddenly came out the front door, walking toward his car.

Deciding that they couldn't risk losing him, they rushed over to the car and grabbed him. Trying to squirm away, Tillo protested that they had the wrong man. "I'm not him! I'm not him!" he screamed.

But, as always, Mackenzie had done her homework and there was no doubt that she had her man—the fugitive that was wanted on charges of rape in Los Angeles, the man who had skipped out on his sentencing and stuck me with a bill of $350,000.

The Seattle cops arrived a few minutes later and Tillo was immediately hauled off to jail.

Calling me immediately after to give me the good news, Mackenzie and I both thought that would be the last we heard from Nour Tillo. I breathed a giant sigh of relief. It was just a matter of the local Seattle authorities notifying the Los Angeles County Sheriffs to pick him up. Our bond would certainly be exonerated when he appeared in court and our indemnitors relieved of their responsibility.

But there was an unexpected twist.

The following day, Tillo appeared in the Seattle court and the judge, ignoring the no bail hold placed by the California court, released Tillo on a $5,000 bond and off he went, on the lam again.

Both Mackenzie and I were furious! After all of her efforts, our fugitive had been carelessly let loose. Which meant I would fail in my obligation to have my defendant show up in court to face the music and once again be responsible for paying the court $350,000.

Mackenzie and I had to go back to the drawing board and figure out a new game plan. I flat-out refused to throw in the towel.

More determined than ever, Mackenzie was back on the hunt and quickly got a lead. Tillo was allegedly on his way to Canada just 100 miles away. Immediately, she alerted the proper authorities of his fugitive status and he was finally apprehended.

The Canadian authorities saw to it that Tillo was returned to Los Angeles to finally face sentencing on his rape conviction. Nour Tillo would eventually serve his time in prison. Justice prevailed.

Everyone was ecstatic that Tillo had been captured, Mackenzie for getting her man, Tillo's partners for not being forced to lose their homes, and me for not having to pay a crushing $350,000 forfeiture.

I was absolutely delighted to pay Mackenzie for her fabulous work. As always, she most certainly earned her twenty percent.

As I wrote out her check for the $70,000 fee, she stopped me before I had finished, my pen still in-hand.

"Chickie … I picked him up twice."

As I began to fully comprehend what she was saying I could barely utter any words.

"Mackenzie, please tell me you aren't going to charge me twice for this one fugitive."

She mulled it over for a few moments. "Well, Chickie, I'll make you a deal. I'll charge you 20 percent for the first pickup and 10 percent for the second."

Sighing deeply, I began writing out a new check for $105,000. It was a steep price to pay but I was comforted with the knowledge that we got our man. A man who would likely cause undue harm toward innocent people had he remained at large.

Tillo's father was not at all happy receiving $95,000 back from Chickie's Bail Bonds instead of the $200,000 cash collateral he had provided, plus that his son had been put away to serve his well-deserved sentence. McKenzie Green was paid twice the largest bounty fee she had ever received for one defendant. Months later I was tickled to see McKenzie featured in *The New Yorker* magazine where she told the story of "the largest fee she had ever received: $105,000."

-22-
CHICKIE'S STING OPERATION

With her thick Italian accent, I could barely understand what Mrs. Giovanni was saying on the phone until she uttered the words, "Please! You must save my daughter!"

It was one of the few nasty days in Southern California, with ominous dark clouds looming in the sky, threatening to unleash a torrential downpour at any moment. In California "rain" is something of a dirty word so I much prefer to use the phrase "liquid sunshine."

The gloomy weather outside made me long for two things: a hot bowl of minestrone and a glass of Chianti—the best antidote for a day like that. There were really only a few decent Italian restaurants near where I lived, but a decision on the matter would have to wait because the phone was ringing off the hook.

"Chickie's Bail Bonds. May I help you?" And then came a stream of words, heavily accented and full of desperation.

"Slow down," I gently coaxed. But the more I asked her to repeat herself and slow down, the more desperate she became.

It must have been two straight minutes of her talking until I heard the plea for me to save her daughter. After some additional back-and-forth, I agreed to meet Mrs. Giovanni that afternoon at her Italian restaurant in Marina Del Rey.

The clouds that earlier had been so menacing had darkened even further. Rain drenched the streets, making the Los Angeles drive even more precarious than usual.

Entering the restaurant, my soaked umbrella in hand, I was greeted by the unmistakable mouth-watering aroma of garlic, tomato sauce, and other Italian delicacies. The cozy ambience was a welcome reprieve from the storm outside. Italian music rang out through the speakers. Traditional, red-checkered tablecloths lay on every table while heavy-set waiters with mustaches scurried around diligently with over-flowing trays.

Mrs. Giovanni rushed over to me, talking a mile a minute in broken English. In true Italian tradition, food always came first. She would not even think about discussing any business with me until she had filled my belly to her satisfaction. Perusing the menu, I spotted the minestrone I had been longing for.

After enjoying my soup, and yes, paired deliciously with a glass of chianti, I had a divine pasta dish and then Mrs. Giovanni insisted I indulge in a delectably rich dessert.

It was only at that point that we could finally get down to business. I encouraged her to explain the dire circumstances to me.

Through intermittent tears, she spoke about the death of her husband who had tragically died from a heart attack one year earlier. Their 16-year-old daughter, Maria, had been extremely close with her father and hadn't fully recovered from the loss. Her behavior had suddenly turned rebellious, and Mrs. Giovanni felt she had lost complete control of her daughter.

Maria had become involved with a young man named Joe Carruthers, recently bailed out of jail.

I began to connect the dots. I knew exactly who Joe was because I was the one who had bailed him out of Los Angeles County Jail. In fact, I had also met Mrs. Giovanni's daughter Maria a few weeks earlier at Dolores Restaurant in West Los Angeles.

Maria was the youngest indemnitor I had ever encountered, although it seemed she was trying to appear much older with her heavily applied makeup, provocative short leather skirt, and flesh-revealing blouse. But it was clear to me that she was just a teenager.

Joe had been arrested for vandalism and was in jail awaiting trial at his "home away from home"—this was certainly not Joe's first run-in with the law. In this instance, Joe had been caught by the police after having knocked over the protective fencing of a residence. The police alleged that Joe had been on the run after smashing several neighborhood car windshields with a baseball bat. There was a bat in his possession at the time of his arrest.

When I met with Maria, she was trying to convince me to post bail for her boyfriend. Her tears seemed authentic as she explained that Joe was not guilty and had to be released in order to prove his innocence.

Although Maria was quite young, I reasoned that she was no different than any other potential client who wanted their loved one released from custody. Who was I to deny her access to her boyfriend?

I felt sorry for Maria and agreed to post bail for her boyfriend Joe. She gave me two pre-paid airline tickets which would serve as my premium and collateral when turned into cash. Nowadays airline tickets are non-transferable, but at that time, airline tickets were considered legal tender.

The tickets just required Joe's signature in order to redeem them. The arrangement was then concluded, the bond posted, and Joe was ultimately released into Maria's wide-open arms.

Being a seasoned veteran of the bail bond industry, I had developed a keen sense for identifying red flags with prospective defendants. There were some that I could tell were going to be problems just by talking to them on the phone.

Any substance or alcohol abuse is a big red flag. In the early years of Chickie's Bail Bonds, a young woman spent several hours trying to convince me that she and her brother—who was being held in custody at the Santa Monica jail—were both trustworthy individuals.

She was fairly convincing. Eventually we met at the jail to complete the paperwork and for me to post the $20,000 bond for her brother. As I sorted through the necessary documents, suddenly Julia blurted out, "I just can't wait until he gets out of there and we can get on the road to Palm Springs."

Palm Springs?!

I stopped writing out the bond, put down my pen, and confronted her. "Didn't you say that first thing tomorrow morning when your bank opens you would be there to take care of the premium and collateral promised?"

She hastily tried to take back her words, but it was too late. I capped my pen, tore up the bond, and left the police station. Julia was no doubt kicking herself for inadvertently revealing her nefarious plans while I patted myself on the back for avoiding what would most likely be a nasty, costly situation.

Mrs. Giovanni told me that after Joe was bailed out, she forbade Maria to see him anymore because he was trouble, refusing to allow him to set one foot in her house. Maria was heartbroken.

Due to the responsibilities of running a busy restaurant, Mrs. Giovanni was often out of the house for a good portion of the day and evening. However, she continued to sense Joe's presence around the house. There were times she was sure she heard his giant white tennis shoes banging around in her dryer. Suffering at the prospect of her daughter being in harm's way or getting pulled into some illegal scheme, Mrs. Giovanni wanted my help getting Joe out of the picture.

Now, she wasn't looking for me to make a "hit" on Joe or anything foolish like that, of course. She wanted to find a legal way to remove him from their lives. Sometimes it only takes one bad decision for a person to have their life ruined, and I didn't want to see a young girl like Maria make that mistake. Being a part of the criminal justice system, I had certainly seen many people go down a dark path simply by getting involved with the wrong people. As a mother, I understood Mrs. Giovanni's concern. Family is everything.

Leaving the restaurant, I gave her my assurance that I would do something to help. As I drove back home the question remained: *What exactly can I possibly do?*

I needed to find a solution by using the law as my guide. After pondering the situation for a while, I realized that I actually had the means of doing exactly what I had promised Mrs. Giovanni.

Joe had not contacted me upon his release from custody to take the necessary steps to redeem the airline tickets, nor had he returned my numerous phone calls.

With that in mind, I knew I had grounds for surrendering Joe back to the custody of the Los Angeles County Sheriff. Sending a client back into custody isn't a standard thing for a bail bond agent to do. Far from it! It is simply not done without "just cause," meaning a reasonable and lawful cause for action.

Joe had breached our contract by failing to sign over the airline tickets and being unresponsive to me. These actions constituted "just cause" and so I knew that it was time to contact a bounty hunter and formulate a plan, one where Mrs. Giovanni would be happy, I would get paid, and young Maria would have a chance at a better future.

The bounty hunter I hired was a wiry little man named Mortimer with a fabulous British accent and a slick mustache. Together we formed a covert plan where I would play a major role—a sting operation.

Since I hadn't been able to get a response from either Joe or Maria, I needed a way of luring them into the trap. And I knew exactly the kind of bait that would do the trick. Money.

I called Maria knowing that she wouldn't answer, and as expected, I got her voicemail. I had planned exactly what to say.

"Hello Maria, this is Chickie from Chickie's Bail Bonds. I still have the pre-paid plane tickets you gave me, but it turns out they are worth far more than what I need. If you and Joe will meet me at the airport, we'll cash in the tickets, and I'll be able to give you some money."

The prospect of receiving any amount of cash was more than enough to reel them in. Soon after I left the voice mail message,

Maria returned my call and we arranged to meet at Los Angeles International airport the next week.

On the appointed day, I arrived at the airport a few minutes early, hovering on the upper level to survey the scene below where the transaction was scheduled to take place.

I spotted Joe and Maria on the lower level, snuggled close together on an uncomfortable-looking bench. Maria's outfit was even more revealing than the previous time we had met, leaving little to the imagination. As Joe stretched his long legs out over Maria, he seemed as tall as an NBA star—at least to me.

Scanning the area intently, there was no sign of my bounty hunter who was supposed to meet me there. I checked my watch. *Where is he?*

A few more minutes ticked by and I began to get nervous. I didn't want Maria and Joe to flee the scene and for me to miss my chance to nab Joe. The couple was already starting to look around suspiciously and I could tell by their body language that they were thinking something was fishy.

When I saw them stand up from the bench, I knew I had to snap into action. I had to make sure to keep them situated there until my bounty hunter arrived.

Racing down the airport steps, I smiled and waved as I approached them. "I apologize for my tardiness!" They seemed happy to see me and not at all suspicious of me as I made idle chit chat with them. Stall tactics. I needed to drag out the time, but I was trying not to make it obvious as to what I was doing.

I placed my briefcase on the bench and slowly opened it, rustling my hands around inside, extracting all sorts of forms. Most of the forms didn't even pertain to the case, but I knew I had to keep them busy. Minutes went by, forms were strewn everywhere across the bench … and still no bounty hunter.

I continued shuffling forms, putting some back in and grabbing new ones. At a certain point, I ran out of papers, but I had to keep the ruse going without arousing suspicion. I had told them that I would "cash in" the plane tickets and give them some of the money, but Mortimer still hadn't shown up. So, I decided to lead them toward the longest line I could find.

The line moved much faster than I would have preferred and we were very shortly next in line for the airline clerk. Time was running out. With no bounty hunter, our sting operation was falling apart.

Miracle of miracles, suddenly my pager went off. (There were no cell phones in those days.) I excused myself from the young couple, leaving them at the front of the line. Then I went to a nearby pay phone attached to a marble pillar.

As I extended a hand out to pick up the receiver, a man poked his head out from behind the pillar.

"We're all set," Mortimer whispered. My bounty hunter had arrived and was ready to take action. It was all so clandestine I felt I was in an old mystery movie. He informed me that I should proceed to the clerk to cash in the pre-paid tickets.

Without looking at him, I nodded—trying not to give anything away in case Joe and Maria were watching closely.

I rejoined the couple at the front of the line and there was no indication from either of them that anything unusual was happening. Just then, we were called forward by the smiling customer service agent. Trying to play it cool, Joe placed his sunglasses on the counter as the lady behind the counter presented some documents for Joe's signature. She took the pre-paid tickets and commenced counting out the money due—all without knowing that she was inadvertently part of a set up.

Just as the last bill was being placed on the counter, a voice boomed behind us.

"Hands behind your back! You are under arrest!"

We all jumped. I don't know who shook more—Joe, Maria, or the unsuspecting airline agent behind the counter. I admit, I was pretty shaken up but I had the presence of mind to reach across the counter and scoop up the pile of cash. That money was rightfully mine and long past due.

Joe was immediately cuffed by a law enforcement official, then read his rights and carted away. It was all too much for young Maria—who collapsed in tears.

I remained in business mode, counting the money and separating out what I was owed for my premium as well as Mortimer's bounty hunter fee.

Maria had made her way to a nearby bench and was sobbing as I approached her. I handed her the remaining cash along with Joe's sunglasses. "Go home, Maria. Your mother is waiting for you."

With my premium collected and my briefcase in hand, I headed for the exit. It was an unusual sequence of events for a bail bond agent, but I felt that I had done right by everyone—even Maria, although she might not have thought so at the time. She was most likely too young to be able to grasp what her mother and I had done for her that day.

When I walked out of the airport, the weather was beautiful. The sun was shining and there wasn't a cloud in sight.

As I entered my car, I had a strange craving for a bowl of minestrone and a glass of Chianti. I turned on the ignition and headed straight to a certain delicious Italian restaurant in Marina Del Rey.

WE'LL ALWAYS HAVE ISRAEL

My sweetheart is 91 years old and he has Alzheimers.

Alzheimers is not just a disease—it is a thief, a robber of memory, dignity, and self, leaving the most capable, incapable.

Each night my sweetheart and I prepare for sleep with a ritual he created. Bob takes my hand, gives it an affectionate squeeze, and brings it to his mouth for a kiss. He reaches for me and places soft kisses on my mouth and asks, "Have I told you lately that I love you?" I tell him that I would love to hear it again and assure him that I love him too. Only then does he release my hand and lay back down preparing for sleep.

Within a minute or two, Bob again turns to me and asks, "Have I told you lately that I love you?" not remembering he had uttered those same words only moments before. How important to him to utter those words, how uncertain of waking in the morning, wanting to leave me with that parting gift.

Good night, sweetheart.

When Bob first mentioned that he was having trouble with his memory, we both thought that it was nothing to be concerned about.

We simply chalked it up to getting older—something that happens to everyone. I've always felt that age was just a number even if my body didn't necessarily agree. I have always been a Pollyanna, tending to look on the brighter side of things. "Oh goody! You only broke ONE leg!"

But watching the doctor put up the images of Bob's brain scan, I started feeling nervous. Dr. Hyman Gross was a highly respected neurologist to whom Bob had referred many patients over the years. Bob knew that he could count on Dr. Gross to provide an accurate diagnosis, comprehensive care, and be sympathetic to the people he treated. On that fateful day, Bob had become the patient.

When he placed images of a normal brain beside Bob's images it was enough to take my breath away. Literally, I felt that I could not even speak—the shocking reality so evident. Bob's scan revealed that his brain was considerably smaller than the brain of a healthy individual and had significantly wider gaps between the tissue with large clouds of gray matter obstructing everything else.

With just one word Dr. Gross confirmed Bob's suspicions and my worst fear. "Alzheimer's."

Sitting there in disbelief, Bob and I gripped each other's hands tight. The feeling of hopelessness began to sink in as I was reminded of the time my late husband Fred was diagnosed with multiple sclerosis—another life sentence of progressive decline with little or no possible cure or relief.

Bob was my entire world and there it was crumbling right in front of me. But there was no crying. No tears. No screaming. All we could do was listen.

Dr. Gross explained that Alzheimer's disease was the most common cause of dementia. It was an insidious disease that slowly destroyed memory and thinking skills. It would eventually eradicate the ability to carry out even the simplest tasks. In its late stages, people with Alzheimer's also could experience changes in behavior and personality

After the grueling explanation of Bob's Alzheimer's and its

prognosis, Dr. Gross recommended that Bob see Dr. Sheldon Jordan, a doctor in Santa Monica conducting a clinical trial on a new drug hoping to delay the progression of this debilitating disease.

When we visited Dr. Jordan, we were informed that there was one spot left in the clinical trial which Bob could now take. After reeling from the dreadful blow of Bob's diagnosis, suddenly there was a faint glimmer of hope.

To celebrate this piece of good news, we immediately drove to one of our favorite restaurants, The Wilshire. There we sat in the bar, holding hands, ordering all the hors d'oeuvres on the bar menu and drinking fruity martinis until the bitter taste of what we had been going through was pushed as far away as possible.

We had to live for the moment because I didn't know how many of those moments we had left. As with Fred's multiple sclerosis, Alzheimer's was frightening in its unpredictability. MS affected the body while Alzheimer's affected the mind. The only predictability of these diseases was their unpredictability.

Countless memories swirled in my head about our wonderful relationship. Would he be able to remember them and cherish them as I do?

Wistfully thinking back on our life together and the special moments we had shared—exciting travel to foreign lands, spectacular meals at the finest restaurants, and an array of social and cultural experiences.

I didn't want our adventures to end.

I was over the moon when Bob took me to Rome. I had always relished the thought of going to Europe and Bob was ever mindful of fulfilling my dreams. With wonderful palaces, thousand-year-old churches, ancient ruins, beautiful statues, and elaborate fountains, Rome had an immensely rich cultural heritage all wrapped up in a cosmopolitan atmosphere.

And there I was, with the love of my life, drinking it all in. Sheer bliss.

Walking back to our hotel one evening, I glimpsed a couple on the other side of the street eating chocolate ice cream cones. I could tell they were Americans as I approached them asking, "May I have a lick?"

They were shocked at first, then shook their heads and laughed. "No, but we'll show you where to get them."

The American couple escorted us to the nearby ice cream store, but before they left, they advised, "Don't sit down. It's more expensive. Just walk up to the counter."

We thanked them for their tip and said goodbye, excited to dig into our own delicious ice cream.

Walking through the lobby of our hotel, someone suddenly tapped Bob on the shoulder. As Bob turned around his eyes widened in surprise. "What are you doing here?"

It was the same American man we had seen earlier with the ice cream cone!

Ed and Barbara Gray were an interesting couple from Connecticut also staying at the Marriott Hotel and on their way to the Sirenuse Hotel in Positano, exactly our destination.

We spent four days with our new friends, having an exceptional time. In that short time, we grew so close that when we left, it felt like we were leaving family. When we said goodbye, they made us promise we would come and visit them.

A couple of months after our trip, Bob had a family reunion in New York. Since we were so close, we decided to drive out to visit our new Connecticut friends. They were delighted to see us and showed us a lovely time.

The fateful coincidences continued. A week or so after we returned home to Los Angeles, Bob received a surprising phone call from his niece. "Uncle Bob, somebody wants to talk to you." A moment later I heard Bob let out a soft chuckle. "Ed, what are you doing with my niece?"

As fate would have it, Bob's niece Susie was married to Ed's cousin. What an amazing thing! A chocolate ice cream cone had led us to a friendship that felt like family and now we learned that they really *were* family. Had I not asked the two strangers on the street for a lick of their ice cream cone, Bob would never have known that part of his family.

Both Bob and I had the travel bug and were always yearning to explore—not surprising when you consider that was how we had met. Over the years, Bob took me on many trips all over the world, introducing me to museums, art galleries, restaurants, and absorbing all facets of international heritage. The world was our oyster.

Ours was a romance that I had never dreamt possible, although perhaps not the most traditional. He truly was unlike any man I had ever met.

I remember being on the phone making reservations for one of our trips when Bob overheard me. The travel agent had asked me a question and I said, "Let me check with my traveling companion."

"Traveling companion?!" Bob blustered. "*That's* what I am? I want to be a fiancé," pounding his fist on the table.

Still holding the phone receiver, I was taken aback that Bob seemed so upset but I didn't say a word, I simply pointed to my naked ring finger.

The message was received and the following week my ring finger was no longer naked—adorned with a beautiful, sparkling diamond ring. Bob had officially become my fiancé—although I couldn't convince him to move in with me. He loved the house he bought after his divorce, close to his Temple, his bakery, and the neighborhood he loved.

We did eventually move in together, but we never

married—enjoying the fact that we are forever each other's fiancé.

Whenever people ask why we weren't married, Bob humorously answered, "We are waiting for parental consent!" The line was always greeted with laughter.

<hr>

There was never one time we were together—not 30 years ago and not now—that Bob wasn't holding my hand or touching me, cementing our relationship—showing his love.

As Bob's condition worsened, sometimes with lightning speed, he would forget things that were such an everyday part of him. As a doctor he was accustomed to washing his hands often, thoroughly scrubbing them before eating and as soon as he finished in the bathroom. My heart would break a little more each time I realized his lifelong habits were becoming things he needed reminding of, no longer a part of who he was.

Speech became more limited as time went on. Talking on the phone, phrases such as, "I love you" and "I miss you" became his sole contributions to the conversation. His family learned to accept this just as I did.

Even today, with all of his limitations, he still asks me several times a day, "Have I told you lately that I love you?"

Each night we cuddle together under our warm comforter. As he nods off to slumber, I lay there, listening to him breathe, thinking how fortunate I am to still have him in my life.

And trying hard not to think of when he will no longer be there.

-24-

ONE MORE CHASE

Although Bob, or Dr. Bob, as he was affectionally called first by his caregivers and then by everyone, received a terrible diagnosis in 2017, we were optimistic when he showed no signs of illness for the first two years. Alzheimer's was known to be unpredictable, showing no signs—until it did.

Bob and I were enjoying living in my newly remodeled home in Manhattan Beach. As much as he loved the house he bought after his divorce, he knew he could no longer live alone. He was no longer driving. The old car he loved sat decaying in the driveway of his house.

Bob was very attached to his home and car. Occasionally we would go visit his "Beverly Hills adjacent" house. It made him happy to be puttering around, trimming the rose bushes that lined the walkway while complaining that the gardener was not doing a good job. The fig tree that always produced lots of fruit seemed sad without him. Even the orange tree stopped producing.

My housekeeper, Mayela, who blessed us with her appearance once a week, was the only help I had in the house until Bob's accident.

Bob showed physical decline before mental. He began walking with a cane and I was advised to get help, that it wasn't safe for me to be fully responsible for him. I interviewed a mother/daughter team of experienced caregivers, or so they said, and hired them. Their first responsibility was to take Bob to our local outpatient lab for his regular blood work.

Fortunately, I was at home when I received the call that Bob had fallen outside the nearby lab. So much for "excellent" care. I rushed over. Bob was somewhat dazed, but the paramedics said he didn't seem to be injured, although they insisted I drive him to the hospital for a full evaluation.

The doctor who admitted Bob to the Santa Monica Hospital told us that he had a slightly fractured bone, but far more distressing was that his sodium was dangerously low and they were shocked at the type of medication he had been prescribed. The doctor explained that Dr. Bob would have been admitted even without the fracture.

The rehabilitation center where Bob was encouraged to go after his hospitalization was wonderful, very professional personnel helping Bob to walk again. As in the hospital, I couldn't bear to leave him alone. I had been with him almost twenty-four hours a day, but I couldn't keep the pace—my health was suffering.

Upon referral, Eddie, an excellent experienced caregiver, became a fixture in our lives. He spent nights with Bob while in rehab so that I could go home to sleep. When Bob was finally released, able to walk again, Eddie accompanied us home and managed his care—helping him shower, preparing his meals, giving me the freedom I needed.

As Bob's Alzheimer's symptoms increased, so did his helpers. He loved Evelyn, a lovely young woman who was great with him. I wanted her to move to Florida with us, but she couldn't leave her family.

My daughter Karen had lived in Clearwater, Florida for many years. We would joke that when I became old, I would move to be close to her. What started as a joke became reality as Bob continued to decline.

Moving wouldn't be easy. I had my son Mitch in LA, not to mention my friends I had made over a lifetime of being an Angeleno, but I knew I needed the support of my daughter and son-in-law, plus my grandson and his wife who also lived in Clearwater. Mitch had always wanted to move to Florida. The challenge was Bob. He had moved from New York to Los Angeles as a young man and here I was trying to pull up those deep roots.

Bob never really agreed to the move. When he saw the giant moving van with all of our belongings on it, he just sat in his walker on our driveway in disbelief.

Over the years every care giver who took care of Bob always commented what a sweet man he was. He never complained about anything. He appreciated our Florida caregivers, Katia in particular, who spent hours singing his favorite Hebrew songs with him. No, Katia is not Jewish, just a wonderful caring person who made certain Bob was happy, singing, reading large print books, or putting together his favorite puzzles of New York and especially Amsterdam where he had studied medicine.

The move was the right thing to do. My family supported me as Bob continued to decline.

Unlike Bob, a true New Yorker, I was raised in Los Angeles and missed lifelong friends like Lorraine whom I had known since nursery school, plus other friends, some of whom had started to decline. I also missed my business associates, all of whom had become friends over the years. I was homesick.

When my family and Bob's caregivers assured me he would be fine in my absence, I invited one of Bob's caregivers, Shelby, who had become a good friend and had never been to Los Angeles, to join me. Off we went, ready for another adventure in LA I should have known then that it wouldn't feel like home without one or two run-ins with fugitives.

First on the agenda was my meeting with my accountant of no less than thirty-five years—after my coffee, of course. I didn't notice that I was missing my phone until I left the café and was getting back in my car to make the meeting. I was not alarmed. How many times over the years had I inadvertently left it in one ladies' room or another? Everywhere from restaurants to hospitals, it was always quickly recovered.

This time was different. My phone had disappeared in a flash; no doubt the person next in line to use the facilities had grabbed it and ran.

With Apple's help, I was able to disable the phone immediately. However, it was my daughter Karen and grandson Marcus back in Florida who were the heroes of my story, to say nothing of my "wheel man," Shelby, who with her amazing driving skills, really saved the day.

Accessing "find my phone," Karen could tell me exactly where my phone was, speeding away from the scene of the crime. Between her and Marcus, we were able to track and follow the speeding vehicle all over Los Angeles.

My phone seemed to develop wings as it flew up Robertson Boulevard through Beverly Hills, zigging and zagging north all the way up to Sunset where it gave chase west past gorgeous estates, eventually turning south onto the grounds of the UCLA campus, touring it fully before dropping into the city of Westwood and finally heading west again to the beach city of Santa Monica.

All of this time, the race car driver in the making, my friend Shelby, was following Karen and Marcus's directions, trying hard to catch up to the elusive driver in possession of my precious phone. Every time we thought we were upon the car, a quick turn would leave us stuck at a red light. But we were close. At one point we caught a glimpse of my phone—a reluctant passenger in a small white vehicle. But we could never get close enough, getting stuck at yet another red light as the car with its special cargo sped through it, leaving us in the dust.

Continuing our tour of Santa Monica, we followed the car through Venice, through Marina Del Rey, never quite catching up as the white car appeared to skedaddle through every signal while we were forced to stop.

More than once I considered giving up the chase, considering finding an Apple Store where all of my precious photos and information could be preserved on a new phone. But my grandson

Marcus was diligent, insisting that the thief could not be allowed to get away with my phone.

After touring Marina Del Rey, I was surprised to find us in the vicinity of the Los Angeles Airport. Marcus's voice was in my ear insisting, "Go, go, go! You're almost on him now!" And my voice, just as adamant, insisting, "We can't keep going. The sign says 'No entrance – keep out! No cars allowed!'"

Of course, Shelby went plowing ahead ignoring the literal warning signs until Marcus told us we had to be right on top of my phone. And right where the dot on the map said my phone should be was a man boarding a blue airport shuttle bus. He had to be the thief. Obviously, he had been dropped off and now had boarded transport to his Jet Blue flight, which would take him and my phone to parts unknown, never again to be recovered!

Marcus was screaming at us to stop the bus before it could get away, carrying my phone with it, an impossibility until fortunately the bus turned slowly toward us. Shelby, following Marcus's insane direction, pulled our car across the front of the bus, blocking its progress.

I can only imagine what the bus driver was thinking as her bus came to a forced halt. Shelby ran over to the driver's window, explaining that her passenger had stolen my phone while I flew to the front exit just in time to block the thief from making his hasty getaway.

Although this burly guy might not have found this little ninety-something Jewish lady very intimidating, he somehow knew I wasn't about to back down. Eyes flashing, hands on my hips, I confronted the man like he was a client who had run out on bail. "You're not going anywhere. You're going to give me back my phone."

He finally confessed that he possibly had seen a phone on a bus seat, and upon my command, retrieved it and handed it to me. On the seat indeed! We both knew it had come directly out of his pocket! Tail between his legs, he returned to his seat on the bus.

Having witnessed this entire exchange, the lovely bus driver exited her vehicle, coming over to our car to tell us how delighted she was that my phone was recovered. She admired what balls it took for our race car driver to pull up crossways in front of her bus, to say nothing of my part blocking the thief from his hasty exit. What's not to like? I had never let any hurdles get in my way of chasing justice. Leaving town and turning ninety was no exception.

Although semi-retired, each time my phone rings I secretly hope it's a new case. A chance to help someone in need. A new opportunity to make a difference.

When the phone rings in the middle of the night, most people panic.

Not me.

I'm hoping that someone, somewhere has decided to Call Chickie—She Comes to You!

EPILOGUE

After three decades it is still an absolute thrill for me to be a part of the bail bond business. Nothing excites me more than being able to speak to one of Los Angeles' top criminal defense attorneys about a new case. I still enjoy talking to a defendant's family for the first time and working out the challenges of their situation—knowing that their loved one will soon be released from custody and reunited with them.

I started late with my career in the bail bond industry, but my success is proof that regardless of a person's age or gender, they can do anything they set out to do.

From the very beginning of Chickie's Bail Bonds, I decided to follow my instincts. I was doing something unheard of at the time, becoming the only bail bond agency devoted exclusively to taking care of the needs of criminal defense attorneys' clients.

Despite all odds being against me, I took a chance and never looked back. I didn't have an office, I didn't have the money to buy fancy ads in the *Yellow Pages*, and yet I dared to venture into the all-male world of bail bonds.

Thrust into the rough and tumble bail bond industry, I never shied away from the fact that I was a woman. Instead, I leaned into all the strengths that being a woman encompassed: patience, empathy, and honesty. Words that weren't usually associated with the much-maligned bail industry. By treating clients with compassion and understanding I gained the respect of all the criminal defense attorneys that I served.

My unique way of looking at the business of bail helped me to elevate it by viewing the accused as a person who made terrible a mistake, rather than a disgusting criminal. I learned to have faith in the justice system that those who were guilty would be convicted and pay for their crimes, and those who wanted to make things right would be given a second chance. Just as I was given a second chance. In my career, in my life, and in love.

Each one of us has a little voice inside that says, "I can do that," about some activity or ability. It's just a matter of listening to that voice and not being overwhelmed by all the minutiae of life. There are so many distractions that make it easy to lose yourself. Concentrate on your potential and what you can bring to the world to make it a better place. Believe in yourself even if no one else believes in you—whether it be your friends, family, or even your own husband.

Many things have changed since I started in the bail bond business. There are far more women in the industry—something I strongly encourage. It's vital for women to fulfill themselves and contribute something to society. We can be an important part of the world, and we shouldn't ever let a silly idea like "that's a man's job" get in our way.

Helping others has always been a hallmark of Chickie's Bail Bonds. There is no more gratifying feeling than making a positive difference in someone's life.

As such, I am going to leave you with some advice, because you never know when you, a family member, or a friend might face a dire situation…

What Do You Do if You or Someone You Love is Arrested

No one plans to get arrested. But even some of the greatest people in history have found themselves on the wrong side of the law, and as I'll remind anyone who will listen, the accused are always presumed innocent until proven guilty.

If you or someone you care about has been placed under arrest, it's always wise to keep a few simple rules in mind to help ensure that you or your loved one is treated fairly.

Rule #1: Keep your mouth shut!

When an arrestee is read his or her Miranda rights as you've probably seen on TV ("Anything you say can or may be used against you in a court of law"), it is serious business even if innocence is certain. Far too many people have loose lips when they are arrested, not realizing that even the slightest inadvertent utterance can come up during a trial and later be presented as incriminating evidence by the prosecuting attorney.

Rule #2: Get the very best criminal defense attorney you can afford.

If you are arrested, your attorney will work diligently to prove your innocence, have the charges against you reduced, or obtain the most lenient sentence possible. Of course, everyone is entitled to a defense and that's where a public defender comes into play. I empathize with people who can't afford to pay a good criminal defense attorney, because although a public defender may likely be a good lawyer, he or she is often one overwhelmed with cases. Therefore, if you have any choice in the matter, I urge you to spend the money.

Rule #3: Follow your attorney's advice.

Your defense attorney has anywhere from years to decades of experience working within the law and assuredly has a much more comprehensive understanding of the particulars of your specific predicament. Regardless of how many shows you have watched on television, once you have an attorney that you feel comfortable with, you should let them do their job. When they tell you to post bail in order to prepare the best defense possible, make sure you use a highly regarded bail agent.

Understanding Bail -
Ten Commonly Used Bail Terms

The law is famously complicated. You may not need a juris doctorate to qualify for a bail bond license, but that doesn't mean that any part of the bail process is simple. As such, there are many technical phrases that may not be immediately clear to the layperson. Furthermore, the process of seeking bail, like many steps in the legal process, is frequently misrepresented in popular culture, and a lot of people may know of some of the terms but may also be misinformed with regard to their precise definitions. Considering this, I've included a brief glossary below to help guide readers.

1. **Bail**: Security demanded by the court to guarantee the appearance of the accused during the pending action while on release from custody.

2. **Bail Agent**: An individual licensed by a state's Department of Insurance who contracts for the undertaking of bail.

3. **Bail Bond**: A power of attorney issued by a surety insurance company, executed by their licensed agent to allow a defendant freedom from incarceration pending adjudication of the criminal case.

4. **Bail Bond Agreement**: The contract between the indemnitor and the bail agent whereby the indemnitor becomes liable for the bail undertaking.

5. **Defendant**: A person required to appear in court to answer pending charges.

6. **Indemnitor**: Friend or family of the defendant who accepts liability for the bail bond by pledging real or personal property.

7. **Liability:** Responsibility for any financial loss incurred in connection with the bail bond posted.

8. **Premium**: The bail bond fee as regulated by the Department of Insurance, typically ten per cent of the bail amount.

9. **Collateral**: Assets pledged by an indemnitor as security for the appearance of a defendant released on a bail bond. Collateral is returned to the depositor upon adjudication of the case.

10. **Own Recognizance** (O.R.): Release from custody by making a personal promise to appear in court on a date mandated by the court.

WORDS TO LIVE BY

FROM CHICKIE LEVENTHAL

My chariot of life
goes flying through time,
while I, at the helm,
grasp tightly the reins
that bind me to life.

When my future is uncertain,
and I can only look at the past,
how fortunate I am,
that I can say, "Oh boy!
Did I have a blast!"

As long as there are
more mountains to climb
I won't be afraid
of old Father Time.

Chickie, at age 17, and her
mother on the beach.

Chickie as Dolly Levi in
The Match Maker.

Chickie as a secretary.

Chickie's husband, Fred.

Fred with Karen, Chickie & Fred's first child.

Karen with Grandpa Joe, Chickie's father.

Chickie as assistant-vice president, Cotton Belt Insurance Company.

Chickie, the business owner.

Mitch and Chickie celebrating 30 years of Chickie's Bail Bonds.

Chickie's daughter Karen, and
granddaughter, Angela, in London.

Chickie and her great nephew,
Kevin Mitnick

Chickie's Bail Bonds staff:
Karen, Mitch, and Chickie.

Chicki and her best friend, Lorraine, celebrating their 70th birthdays.

George Cameron and daughter Verlene at Chickie's 25th anniversary holiday party.

Chickie addressing guests at her annual holiday party.

Attorney Robert L. Shapiro.

Chickie & Attorney Shapiro.

Chickie with attorney
Brad Brunon.

Chickie with Attorney
John Yzurdiaga

Chickie with Her Honor Ana Ho.

Dr. Bob In the backyard
of Manhattan Beach in
Chickie's flower garden.

Chickie and Dr. Bob at a
Los Angeles fundraiser.

Chickie and Dr. Bob
celebrating 30 years of
Chickie's Bail Bonds.

Chickie and Dr. Bob in 2019.
Photograph by Steven Cohn.

Volume 33, Number 22 — THE COMMUNITY OF BUSINESS — May 30 - June 5, 2011 • $3.00

LOS ANGELES BUSINESS JOURNAL

UP FRONT

A Big Star For Those Behind Bars

Bail bond expert built her career on working with celeb clientele.

Your average L.A. crime suspect has all manner of gritty bail bond companies to call. But who do celebrities and other high-income types call?

It may well be Chickie Leventhal of **Chickie's Bail Bonds** in Manhattan Beach. If she bails you out, she'll probably be wearing her trademark rose-tinted glasses. Just don't tell her she looks like your mom's bridge partner.

"I don't believe I give the image of being a grandmother," said Leventhal.

She has bailed out rapper Snoop Dogg, Girls Gone Wild creator Joe Francis and actor Tom Sizemore. Leventhal's clients are referred by the 75 or so high-profile lawyers who have come to know her. That was the case when she bailed out Phil Spector, who was eventually convicted of killing model Lana Clarkson.

"I had no idea who he was," she said. "But I said, 'Of course,' because Robert Shapiro was asking."

After Leventhal climbed the ranks in an insurance firm in the 1980s, where the company wrote policies for bail-bond businesses, she decided to start her own shop for bail bonds.

She knows to take money and other valuables to ensure the bailee shows up at court. For example, when one client wanted to post bail for his mistress, Leventhal knew what to take: his wife's phone number.

She's now considered an authority on bail. She recently gave a lecture to the Los Angeles Superior Court Bail Bond Committee, comprising Los Angeles County judges, about the workings of her practice.

– Jonathan Polakoff

RINGO H.W. CHIU/LABJ

Reclining Type: Leventhal at Manhattan Beach home.

Los Angeles Business Journal interviews
Chickie in her backyard.

ACKNOWLEDGMENTS

Those to whom I am grateful extend far before the creation of my book.

Without the encouragement and help of George Cameron, bail agent extraordinaire, I would never have taken on the creation of Chickie's Bail Bonds which ultimately led to my writing this book.

When I expressed doubt about starting a business, my very dear friend Ron Letvin said, "Chickie, if I were looking for a partner in my business, it would be you." Words that gave me the courage to go ahead with this foreign concept of starting my business.

When my dear friend Margie Finn looked at my first attempt at writing, she was tempted to run and hide, but she stayed with me, helping me, teaching me, and encouraging me. God Bless Margie.

My dear friend Sue Ganz-Schmitt, a published author, read my attempt to write my story. Full of encouragement, she introduced me to her good friend, Kelly Sullivan Walden, writer and entrepreneur extraordinaire who, along with Sue, created TEAM CHICKIE, rooting for my success with all their hearts—all but the pom-poms.

It was Kelly who introduced me to Thea Rademacher, owner of Flint Hills Publishing, who took a chance on an unknown author and published my book. With Thea's enormous heart, expertise, and patience, she made my dream a reality, for which I will be eternally grateful.

Acknowledgment wouldn't be complete if I did not acknowledge the friends and wonderful family who encouraged me, especially my Dr. Bob, who always let me know how proud he was of me.

ABOUT THE AUTHOR

Growing up in the melting pot of Boyle Heights in East Los Angeles during the 1930s and 40s, Chickie enjoyed school with many children who were different from herself: Mexicans, Blacks, and Asians. Learning early on that the differences she perceived were only on the outside prepared her for a career of helping people of all races and creeds.

Working as a secretary for many industries introduced Chickie to the world of bail bonds which led to her establishing the first female-owned bail bond agency in Los Angeles. For 37 years, she worked with the most respected Los Angeles criminal defense attorneys, providing bail bonds for their clients—always with consideration and respect—thus endearing her to all with whom she worked.

Chickie wrote her book with multiple purposes in mind: to entertain and enlighten the reader; to dispel negative impressions surrounding the bail bond industry; and to encourage women of all ages not to be afraid to follow their dreams. Fifty years old when she created Chickie's Bail Bonds in order to support her family when her husband became ill, Chickie reminds us, "If I could do all of that and write a book about it with only a high school diploma, so can you!"

www.flinthillspublishing.com/authors/chickie-leventhal